GIVE ME THIS MOUNTAIN

Reverend C.L. Franklin

GIVE ME THIS MOUNTAIN

Reverend C. L. Franklin

Life History and Selected Sermons

Edited by Jeff Todd Titon

Foreword by Jesse Jackson

University of Illinois Press
Urbana and Chicago

This book is printed on acid-free paper.

Portions of the Preface, Introduction to the Sermons, and Afterword, and the sermon *A Mother at the Cross* appeared in the *1987 Folklife Annual,* published by the American Folklife Center, Library of Congress.

Library of Congress Cataloging-in-Publication Data

Franklin, C. L. (Clarence LaVaughn), 1915–1984.
  Give me this mountain: life story and selected sermons/C.L.
Franklin; edited by Jeff Todd Titon.
     p. cm.
  ISBN 0-252-01018-3 (cloth : alk. paper). ISBN 0-252-06087-3 (paper :
alk. paper)
  1. Franklin, C. L. (Clarence LaVaughn), 1915–1984. 2. Afro-
American Baptists—Biography. 3. Baptists—United States—Clergy—
Biography. 4. Baptists—Sermons. 5. Sermons, American.
I. Titon, Jeff. II. Title.
BX6455.F73A3 1989
286'.1'0924—dc19
  [B]   89-4649
                                                                        CIP

Contents

Foreword

Clarence LaVaughn Franklin, the high priest of soul preaching, affectionately called "the Rabbi," "the learned one," preached my ordination sermon in 1968 at the Fellowship Missionary Baptist Church in Chicago where Reverend Clay Evans is pastor. He connected the dry bones in the valley and with eloquent and delicate transition, he moved with Ezekiel into the wheel in the middle of the wheel. One wheel, chronos, man's history: the ghettos, *los barrios,* the sumptuous and the suppressed of man's history. One wheel, the nation's history. And then, kyros, God's wheel of history. I still try to keep the wheels in perspective. I still try to preach to the bones in the valley, the despised, the damned, the disinherited, the disrespected, and I realize at my extremities stands God's opportunity. Thus when my preaching falls on deaf ears, and it appears that my salt has lost its savor, I still say, "Lord God, thou knowest."

C. L. Franklin was a prophet. C. L. Franklin was rare, not just unique; famous because he was well known, but great because of his service. C. L. Franklin, the most imitated soul preacher in history, a combination of soul and science and substance and sweetness.

Did not our ears perk up for years before we had a television or an elected official in America, if we could just hear WLAC, Nashville, Tennessee, Randy's, on a Sunday night? Sunday night, New Bethel, Hastings Street, was the common frame of reference for the black church. The soul of Motown was Hastings Street before Grand Boulevard. And from that plateau he shared his broader ministry. It was out of this womb and web that Aretha Franklin was spawned. She was no accident, but rather a product of Providence. The acorn does not fall far from the tree.

The great modern-day evangelists and revivalists—Jasper Williams,

Clay Evans, C. L. Moore, Caesar Clark, and Donald Parsons and all the others—there's a little C. L. Franklin in our throats if we have that talent, or in our hearts if we are possessed with the urge to preach. We still hear them say, "Well, he reminds me a little bit of C. L. Franklin." C. C. Coleman once said that "Before C. L. starts that breathing thing, and that singing, you've been well preached to."

A genius at homiletics, exegesis, and delivery, he was a guiding force in the historic Civil Rights Movement in 1963. He helped to lead the March on Detroit which preceded the March on Washington. The record shows him locked arm-in-arm with Dr. King in that march. He challenged the church to be relevant and asked the Lord to give us this day our daily bread. I stood with him the night Coleman Young was declared winner in this city.

C. L. Franklin gave youth a chance. I was speaking in this pulpit as a member of Dr. King's staff before I was ordained. And so Erma and Cecil and Carolyn and Aretha—we're family.

C. L. Franklin was born in 1915, fifty years after slavery, and fifty years before we had the right to vote. He was born in poverty; poverty could not stop him. He was born in segregation. It was illegal for a black man to get an education. No public accommodations, no right to vote, blacks on chain gangs. No friend in the White House, no member of Congress, no black mayor. Born in poverty. But when God wants a flower to bloom, no drought can stop it. His flower did blossom. And so we say thank you for a petal, for an insight, for a song, for a sermon. When the eagle stirred its nest, the flower blossomed.

Reverend Jesse L. Jackson

Preface

Early in the morning of June 10, 1979, three men and two women parked a white 1967 Chevrolet outside the home of the Reverend C. L. Franklin, pastor of Detroit's New Bethel Baptist Church and father of singer Aretha Franklin. The men broke in, apparently trying to steal some antique lead glass windows. Franklin was awake, probably watching television. Hearing them, he took a pistol and went out to the landing. The burglars shot him in the knee and groin. As he fell, the burglars escaped. Hours later, a neighbor found Franklin on the landing. Unconscious and in critical condition, he was taken to a hospital. He remained in a light coma without life-sustaining apparatus for five years, until he died on July 27, 1984. Ministers throughout the United States came to Detroit to pay tribute, and Jesse Jackson preached the eulogy. His funeral was the largest that the city has ever seen.

Some claimed that Franklin was shot over a drug deal. Many were jealous of Franklin's wealth and reputation as the most popular black, Baptist preacher of his generation. But Franklin (1915–84) was not a cult-figure like Daddy Grace, Prophet Jones, or Malcolm X. Instead, his fame rested solidly on pulpit preaching. His Detroit congregation numbered more than ten thousand; dozens of his sermons had been issued on record albums and sold millions of copies; and, with gospel groups that included Aretha, he went on preaching tours throughout the United States. It is said that every African American preacher either has imitated him or has tried to avoid doing so.

Franklin's sermons flow from a rich African American literary, cultural, and religious tradition. For, although he was a learned man and attended both seminary and college, he "whooped," or chanted, in an old-fashioned, extemporaneous black ministerial mode, without manuscript or notes. Combining oratory with intoned poetry, he reached both head and heart. Imaginatively narrating biblical events, locked with his shouting congregation in a driving, rhythmic embrace, his "whooping" climaxed each sermon in a musical ecstasy of communal, ritual drama. In so doing, preacher and congregation affirmed the felt presence of the divine and holy, nurturing trust in themselves and God.

This is a selection from a two-volume work forthcoming from the University of Illinois Press that presents and interprets Franklin's life and sermons. Designed for the millions who were touched by Franklin during his lifetime, this book offers highlights from his life history and prints twenty of his best sermons. Introductions to the life history and sermons explain their arrangement, and an Afterword briefly reviews the African American sermon tradition and Franklin's place in it.

Acknowledgments

Bill Lucas, Sam Jenkins, Sylvan Barnet, Dennis Tedlock, Robert Pinsky, Ken Irby, Leon Forrest, Alan Lomax, Albert Lord, Judy McCulloh, Bess Hawes, Bob Laughton, Alan Jabbour, and T. J. Anderson, friends and colleagues, took a special interest in Reverend Franklin, his sermons, and this project, and I've appreciated their encouragement and help along the way.

Dorothy Swan, Fannie Tyler, Thomas Shelby, Rev. J. H. Porter, Rev. Nathaniel Burks, Rev. Kenneth Moseley, Jackie Vaughan III, Rev. Jim Holley, Rev. T. C. Simmons, and Carolyn Kirkpatrick kindly aided me in my research in Detroit.

Rachel Franklin told me about her son's childhood and her family's history; Erma Franklin generously arranged for me to look through her father's papers and copy what I needed, and she spoke movingly about what it was like for her and her sisters and brother to grow up in a household with so celebrated a father. I'm most grateful to Reverend C. L. Franklin himself for welcoming me into his church, allowing me to tape-record and videotape his sermons, and for the many hours we spent in conversation together.

For fellowships, grants, and institutional support for this project I thank the National Endowment for the Humanities, the National Endowment for the Arts, the Howard Foundation, the W. E. B. Du Bois Institute (Harvard University), Tufts University, and Brown University.

Life History of Clarence LaVaughn Franklin

I edited Franklin's life history from some thirty hours of tape-recorded conversations we had in 1976, 1977, and 1978. We ranged over many topics: his boyhood, his conversion experience and gospel call, his life in the ministry, his opinions on education and politics, his duties as a preacher and pastor, and his remarkable recording career and preaching tours. I removed most of my questions and comments, except those that seemed unusually leading. Extra space between paragraphs signals a break to a different part of our conversations. Where friends and family members' statements amplified or contextualized Franklin's, I included them in endnotes. Occasionally I put in a clarifying word, and I took out false starts and repetitions; but, as Franklin spoke deliberately, I scarcely had to change anything he said. I showed him a draft of the life history in 1979; he made some minor corrections and then approved it. His daughter Erma, reading it some years later, said she could hear his voice throughout.

I couldn't go back any further than my grandparents, because, as you know, during the slave situation families were separated. The children went one way, the parents another. Now my mother's mother was Willie Ann Pitman, and my grandfather was a black preacher, Elijah J. Pitman. Of course there was not too much account for him as a preacher. Mother simply told me that he was preaching immediately after slavery if not in slavery.

So. I was born in Sunflower County, Mississippi, in the rural area near Indianola, on January 22, 1915. I grew up in another rural community outside of Doddsville, Mississippi. My father went off to war, World War I, when I was quite a child. I guess he was drafted; I don't know what the situation was in the military at that time. But he went off to war. He came back at a time that I vaguely remember him. I recall him dressed in his uniform and playing with us, teaching us how to salute, and things of that sort that had to do with the military. I say us, I mean me and my sister who was a year and six months younger, and who, incidentally, is dead now: Louise. But I guess having seen the big cities and having ridden on the ocean liners and having gone to Paris, my father wanted no more of the farm situation—the Southern farm situation at least. And of course he left. And this is the last that we heard of him.

My mother married again in this same rural community near Doddsville. We came up in our stepfather's name, Franklin.[1] There was one child born to that union: Aretha, for whom my daughter is named.

I remember one thing that stands out from after my mother remarried. My father used to go to the commissary. The boss owned the commissary, and he would get his groceries there. The boss would charge him against the crop. Now my father, like many of the sharecroppers, was completely illiterate, to the point that he couldn't even write his name. And of course not being able to read or figure except a bit in his own head, he never really knew what we owed. At the end of the year, which they called on the farm *settling time*, families would total up, and the boss would total up the bales of cotton that had been gathered. Now in our case if we made twenty to twenty-five bales of cotton during the year, the boss would say, "Well, Henry, you didn't come out. But we'll just call it even and start fresh next year."

Now this went on year after year.

I remember Christmas morning. My mother would cry because the only things that she could purchase for the children were raisins and oranges and apples and striped candy. No toys. I never had toys. But I was very anxious about Christmas morning, even to get the oranges and the apples, the raisins and candy. I never will forget that striped candy. (Laughs.)

And that stands out: her crying.

We stayed near Doddsville for a few years, and I went to school there. The school situation that existed there I think was deliberately designed, where the whites controlled the educational system, as well as everything else, to the point where well-established, well-equipped schools were built for the whites, and to keep the blacks backward, they would let the blacks hold their schools in the black churches, where you would have space something about the size of our dining room—not quite as well appointed. (Laughs.) And all of the classes were in that same room.

The teachers were selected, and most of them had not finished grammar school. This was a deliberate attempt to keep the children backward. And of course years later the federal government stepped in, and made certain demands that the teachers had to have at least two years of college, working towards a college degree, which ultimately changed that situation.

But I am aware that it did exist. I lived with it. The white kids were bused to their schools. The black kids walked seven and eight miles to their schools. And some of the bigoted drivers, if it rained and the black kids were walking along the road, they would deliberately hit those water puddles to splash water on the blacks while the kids would be calling out derogatory names like "Nigger, nigger! Coon, coon!" at the black kids.

My first day of school was uneventful. I was familiar with the school grounds in the church and the situation, and I knew most of the children by seeing them every Sunday. Learning to read and write was quite interesting. The state provided books that were brought in mostly from white schools. Most of them were in pretty good shape. My mom could read and write. She didn't make much effort to teach us at home, but she would insist upon us going to school at the time that was provided.

Eventually we moved to Bolivar County, in a rural area near Cleveland, Mississippi. I was about nine years old at the time. We had a little better school there. I remember a professor who we had—I believe he finished Jackson College—and he made a very serious effort to engage and interest the young people in learning. He devised all kinds of methods to engage one's interest. I remember one thing in particular. He would delegate certain boys to keep the order. That would enlist them and their interests, and give them some kind of feeling of being part of the system. And he would take the boys out, walk and talk about agriculture, and talk about various things that we had not seen or heard about.

I remember one time they had a little exercise at school. The teachers had given us each a speech to memorize. This was a frequent sort of thing. You were called upon by your teacher to recite certain poems or speeches, mostly in class but also at a school exercise. And I got on the stage to speak and my sister did likewise, but the kids were noisy. There were many parents there, but the kids were nevertheless noisy, and of course we could hardly be heard.

So my mother waited until we got out of our clothes when we got back home, then got that strap: "The next time you speak, people are going to hear you!"[2]

I liked school, but I was helping with the farm, and I couldn't go until after the crops were finished—maybe the first of December. And of course I had to come back out when farming started again in the middle of March.

We lived on a plantation in Cleveland where my father became a renter. Our house was in a kind of neighborhood, mostly black, but some white sharecroppers too. The house had a kitchen and three bedrooms. No living room. We took our meals in the kitchen, all sitting around a table. Had a cookstove that burned wood. Flour and sugar were stored in a little chest on the wall. The bedrooms had chests of drawers, mirrors, beds. There was a fireplace, an open hearth where we could put on small logs and start a fire. That would be sufficient heat. But we had outdoor plumbing, and that was cold in the wintertime. Outside we had a front porch and a back porch, and a pump for water.

We had a phonograph in one of the bedrooms, a windup floor model. We had blues records—singers like Blind Lemon Jefferson, Roosevelt Sykes. There was a man named Gates[3] who preached something about a dead cat on the line. I heard other sermons of his but I remember that one. Those were records that were generally circulated in the South.

Was there any conflict between blues and the church?

Not within me; I always liked blues. There were some people, some church people who didn't approve it, blues, but they didn't understand that it was part of their cultural heritage. It was just something evil, wicked, according to their thinking, because they'd been taught that.

One year we moved from Cleveland to a little place east of Boyle, Mississippi, and my daddy made a tremendous corn crop and a tremendous cotton crop. And it seemed that at the end of the year there was some dissatisfaction on the part of the renter we were sharecropping with. This man was named Pennington. He was poor, white but poor, as there were many poor whites in the area. My daddy was sharecropping with him, and it was obvious that we were supposed to come out ahead. And there was some dissatisfaction, so this man got his sons and then he sent for his son-in-law to come to augment his forces in the event that any trouble broke out.

This son-in-law had a reputation for killing blacks, and of course he felt that this would frighten my father. And it was just a question of "No, you just didn't make it." No settlement or anything. So at night my daddy would get the sideboards way up on the wagon, and take all of his corn away at night back to where we had formerly lived, Cleveland. He went back to the same place, same house, same man. And this man, a Mr. Casbury, was better. Kind of a Northerner, a banker. He was a bit more generous and fair.

My family didn't do too much except to farm and go to church. On Saturdays we would go on horses and wagons to Cleveland, get there about 12 noon, then walk up and down the same street, because they had only one line of stores. It was more or less a gathering place for most of the blacks and whites on Saturdays. The grocery stores were not segregated, but the restaurants were. You had to go find the black community to go into a restaurant. There was nothing for me to do but stand around and talk to other kids and maybe some grown-ups. I liked to play ball, I liked to shoot marbles with the other boys,[4] I liked to ride, and I liked to go berry hunting, blackberries mostly. Of course there were no recreational facilities for blacks. Occasionally we would go to a picnic, a picnic that mostly was provided by the whites through certain blacks. The whites would give certain blacks so many hogs that had been killed and prepared, and chickens and different foods that you would ordinarily find at a picnic. Certain blacks would prepare it and supervise. It was a common practice in that connection as well as in others. Some of the foremen were blacks who supervised for whites.

Did the whites have anything to do with the black churches?

No. They would possibly provide them for the blacks on the plantations. Now the whites didn't come to the churches except on rare occasions. If there was something special that they wanted to tell the blacks, then they would come. But ordinarily it was totally black.

Segregation was something that was understood by all blacks. I grew up with it. Parents told you that certain things you could do and certain things you couldn't, by being black. These were things that were set aside for white people and blacks had to stay over here. I did have one or two white friends. Mostly the white kids would socialize with the blacks as long as they were kids; there wasn't too much difference.

But when they got to their early teens, then if you went to the white people's house, they would begin telling you to call him "Mr. Jesse," call her "Miss Ann." I did it. And the others did it. And the whole attitude of the young lady or young man changed from that point on. I'm sure they had been instructed themselves.

It didn't really shock me. If from the point of realization when things begin to dawn on you, you're being instructed by your own parents about what the situation is between blacks and whites, and where your place is, and where his place is, I guess when you grow up with that, it doesn't shock you. We had our rationale prior.

My father didn't go to church very much, but my mother was an ardent churchgoer. As far back as I can remember, I was going to church with her. I admired my father, loved him, and all that, but as far as his non-churchgoing, no. He felt all right about the church; he just didn't go. He was just an honest, hardworking man.

The church was central in most black Southern people's lives. For me, not understanding any more than I did understand at the prebaptismal period, it was more or less social; it was somewhere to go after being in the field all week. Going to church Sunday, I met other young people that I knew. The social aspect of it attracted me then; afterwards it began to take on religious significance.

Was there a period when you felt you were under conviction?

I never felt really condemned by God. I never felt that God had something against me. It seemed to me that God had provided all of the things *for* me, including his love, and now it was time to respond. My conversion was more or less typical among black people. I was about nine or ten years old at the time. They had annual revivals at our church in Cleveland, St. Peter's Rock Baptist Church. It was a large church, the largest black church in town. Must have had about six or seven hundred people. It was a wooden building, and quite nice. Wood pews, regular pews, and a choir stand, and a large choir.

On this particular occasion I took a seat on the mourners' bench at the front. Preceding the sermon the people came up to the mourners' bench, and the mourners or prospective candidates got on their knees. One person prayed out loud, and others simply bowed with the one that prayed, and along with the mourners.

My conversion was not unusual or spectacular. When the minister finished his sermon and invited us to come, I simply got up and went to the altar. There were a lot of people who adhered to the tradition of black people; some were rather expressive, shouting and what have you, crying and going on. And some were not.

I had had no dreams or visions. I'd thought on joining the church, but it was during the minister's sermon that I decided now was the time. I felt moved, I felt inspired, and so I went forward with some of the other youngsters. We took the seats that were provided for those who felt they were converted.

The testimonies concerning conversion varied. Some people were very lucid and expressive, and some simply stated, "I feel that I am converted, and I want to join the church." If a person wanted to elaborate on the conversion, people would listen to him, the minister would listen and hear him out, and then propose to the congregation for their membership, and then vote. He was simply taken on his testimony.

So the minister asked me, "Have you taken this seat because you feel you are converted?"

"Yes."

"Do you really believe in God, with all of your heart, your soul, mind, strength?"

"Yes."

And then I was voted in.[5]

The economic situation at the time made it almost impossible for one church to support a pastor, because if the pastor got forty dollars, forty-five, even fifty, he had a good church, according to his thinking. Some of them wouldn't get that much, but they expected it. But he couldn't live on forty or forty-five a month, so he'd travel from one place to the other, from this church to the next. Usually the ministers had four churches and were at a different church every Sunday. But if a funeral arose or somebody were seriously ill, they would come.

The Sunday morning that the pastor came, the time was set, about nine o'clock, for the baptismal service. Mine was a week after the revival. We got in cars or trucks or what have you, and went about eight or ten miles to the Sunflower River. The minister and deacons had previously gone out into the river and set stakes to indicate that you were not supposed to go any further.

The members of the church were lined up on the riverbank, singing. The minister talked on the subject of baptism, the validity of baptism, the necessity of baptism, the tradition of baptism, and so forth. The deacons and pastor were out in the water, receiving the candidates as they marched out. And the pastor baptized us one by one.

It so happened in my case that I went off and left my clothes at the church, and had to come back in the wet robe all the way to the church. A white robe.

Not long after I joined the church I became a member of the choir. I would work all day and walk two miles to the church to practice. We didn't read music; it was all picked up by ear, and we memorized the words. I began in the tenor section, and eventually I evolved into a solo singer. I would go to prayer meetings, testimonial meetings, regular pastoral services.

Did you testify a lot?

No, I didn't do too much testifying.

When I became twelve or thirteen years of age I began thinking about girls. Seeing them at rehearsals and at church. Started thinking about girls.

There was one other thing I thought about seriously. I couldn't see any future in farming. My father was never a successful farmer in terms of economics. There were other people that I could contrast with him, a few successful farmers who owned land, who had cars and trucks, but my father never reached that point. And I had grown up on a farm and I didn't particularly like farming. I was good at farming but I didn't like it after I reached my teenage level and onward.

One night I was standing in the back of our church, with a cap rolled up in my hand, and the president of our State Convention, the late Dr. Benjamin J. Perkins, preached on a passage dealing with Thomas, the disciple Thomas, who doubted the resurrection of Jesus. And his sermon was so vivid and clear to me, and so impressive, that from that night forward, I really felt that I was called to preach.

That was my first known impression. The feeling gradually intensified that I was "called to preach," as it was called then. I was called to preach, meaning that I had a deep conviction that I was supposed to preach. I felt that God was the source of that. I felt impelled.

I remember the minister that inspired me, Dr. Perkins, used to tell a story about the man that inspired him. He said that there was a baptismal service on a river one Sunday, and the deacons had taken the stakes out and put them down so as to keep them from going off a deep end; they could go to these stakes and no further. And he said that just as they were taking out a candidate to be baptized, that a dark cloud came over and that the rain just began to pour. And this minister—I think his name was Reverend Cleveland—stopped and prayed, and told the Lord, "Unveil Sol." And he said that in the course of the prayer, the clouds just dispersed.

Reverend Perkins was a boy then. He was in the congregation by the riverbank.

One night I was in my room, lying on my bed, and I had a dream, or a vision. I wasn't awake at the time. The walls of the room were made of planks, and it seemed that one plank only was on fire, but it didn't consume the house. A voice spoke to me from behind the plank and said something like, "Go and preach the gospel to all the nations." I went and told my mother what I had seen and heard.[6] She was very pleased, and she gave me encouragement.

I went to the church and told them that I felt that I was called to preach. A couple of months later they gave me a trial sermon. I had been thinking about what I wanted to preach about: "I must work the work of him that has sent me while it is day."

It was summertime. I remember delivering it. I imagine it wasn't too well constructed, because I had no training for it. I just spoke about what I felt. I was nervous when I got up before the people and began to preach, but afterwards, as they listened and responded, I felt good, I felt encouraged. When it was over, the people came up to me and complimented and encouraged me.[7] I was about fifteen or sixteen years old.

I recall when I got to Cleveland, I'd be out chopping cotton, or picking cotton, or plowing, in a field that ran right up to the railroad track. Just across the railroad track was the 61 highway. And it was meaningful to me—quite an experience as contrasted with my experience in Sunflower County—to see the trains coming from Memphis enroute to New Orleans and Jackson. The people would be waving out of the windows at us in the field. And cars going down the highway with different license plates from New York and New Jersey and the District of Columbia, Virginia, and Connecticut, and wherever. It gave me a deep longing to someday see these places where the cars came from, where the train came from, and where the people *on* the trains came from.

In the cotton fields of the South they would tell stories that were inspiring and hopeful, about this situation and that situation. They were great storytellers.

Do you remember any?

I recall one. It was when Jack Johnson[8] was the world champion. They used to refer back to that. After Jack Johnson got to be the world champion he was driving from Chicago to St. Louis in some kind of powerful car. And he was driving at very high speed, and the highway patrol had some difficulty catching up with him. When they did catch him, they told him he was fined two hundred dollars.

Jack Johnson said, "Well, take five, because I'm coming back the same way!" (Laughs.)

How do you interpret that story?

Well, these black field hands identified with Jack Johnson. They identified hopefully with his success and possibly their own or the success of their children. And therefore they kept these stories alive. And later they identified with Joe Louis.

I heard stories about Henry Ford and Rockefeller. Rockefeller declared that he had so much money that he had estates here and there, yachts, mountain cabins, country homes, etcetera. And he was talking to Henry Ford about it. And somehow they seemed to have sided with Henry Ford more so than they did with Rockefeller. Maybe because many of them had begun to work for Henry Ford. And Henry Ford said to Rockefeller, "Show me all of this property you have, and I'll buy it and then I'll fence it in—with money!" (Laughs.)

At sixteen I ran away and went to an aunt's place in Shelby, Mississippi, and stayed there for nearly a year. I was within fifty miles of my home, but things weren't too much better, so I went back home to Cleveland.

I had an uncle who had been in contact with some white man in Missouri. He wanted migrant farmers. So I begged my mother to let me go with him. My parents agreed to let me go, so he had a man to come down with a truck to drive us back to Missouri, and I got on the truck with my uncle and his family, another uncle, and we rode to Missouri.

This was the first time I had ever been to Memphis, and I was living no more than a hundred miles from Memphis all these years. We got to Memphis on this trailer-truck, and I was riding along standing between the trailer and cab. Going up one of those hills the truck jackknifed, and I jumped off just in time.

So we went on, to Carruthersville, Missouri. The man provided a tin-top house for us. A lot of noise was made whenever it rained or sleeted, and sometimes it rained in through the cracks where the tin had rusted out. In Cleveland we had a house with wood shingles. All that winter I worked wearing boots, wading in water, pulling in cotton, burrs and all, putting them in the sack, while the sack was floating on the water, the icy water, and sometimes my feet would get numb.

Later I was working for a man using a stalk-cutter, that instrument that went over the field cutting down the stalks of the previous year's cotton. And finally I lost my job because occasionally I would just stop the mules and get off the stalk-cutter and go to preaching. I guess I must have been preaching to myself! And the man fired me.

I stayed in Missouri about a year, and then the next fall I joined another migrant group from Carruthersville to Fulton, Kentucky. We went up there about the first of December. The guy who was driving the truck had so many people on it that we had to stand up in the back of the truck all the way. We asked him for $2 each to have some food on the road. He couldn't find his money, so we spent that whole day without food. We got to Kentucky about nine o'clock that night, and it so happened that this white guy who wanted the migrant hands had food. We stayed there until April or May of the next year.

I remember one night in the barn where we were living there were many church people involved. And on Sunday nights they would have services. And one night they asked me to preach. I was frightened and I went out in the back and prayed. Looked toward the stars and prayed for God to help me. And I did pretty good, pretty good.

Then after Kentucky we went to Benton Harbor, Michigan, and started working for some Germans, picking strawberries. And in each case, starting from Kentucky, all the migrant farmhands lived in tobacco barns, slept on hay.

I was able to clear a little money from these trips, but not much. After that I came back south to Arkansas and stayed with relatives, and then I went back to my home and family in Cleveland.

When I came back home after my migrant work I was at St. Peter's Rock, preaching occasionally. I was about seventeen or eighteen when they ordained me. They had a presbyteria of ministers, pastors, who formed a council. They set a date and I became a candidate. They fired questions upon me having to do with the meaning of baptism, the meaning of prayer, the role of the preacher, the articles of faith, and so forth. They ordained me and I became an associate minister at St. Peter's Rock.

They had what they called *preaching rallies*. Four or five of us, young fellows who had started in the church or who were members of other churches, and each of us would get up and preach a short sermon, one trying to outdo the other.

I went off to a little place called Tutwiler, Mississippi, to preach. And I had been invited to come, and then I was temporarily accepted as the pastor of this church, County Line Baptist Church.

However, there was an element of opposition in the church against me becoming the pastor because the former pastor had been a man of some stature. And in contrast, I was quite young and inexperienced, and some of the opposition had taken that into consideration, noted that.

So they made a motion that I would be elected to carry out the rest of the year, a year's tenure. But there was no real year's tenure. The pastor had been elected to the pastorate of the church on the basis of as long as he and the church could agree; so he had been there for several years. Consequently there was no annual tenure. But this particular person who made the motion and who had his people organized to follow and support his motion, knew what he was doing, and he presumed, and his presumption was right, that the other people didn't understand. So he injected this tenure thing into the election. So I wrote them concerning that, and this man got the letter, and of course he didn't bring up the letter to the congregation.

Well, I went there on the second Sunday in January, which was a little past my year's end. I had been preaching there about six months. They had in the meantime invited another preacher to be there on that Sunday; this opposition. With my lack of experience I didn't really understand how to deal with the problem from the parliamentarian standpoint, so I went in on Saturday, so that the people who were around the little village would know I was in town. I shook hands with some of the people who knew that I wasn't supposed to be there, but no one told me.

The churches in the rural districts usually have a special deacon where the pastor stays all the time, whenever he comes for that monthly Sunday. And I went on out to Deacon Love's house, whose house was the house where I was supposed to stay, Deacon and Mrs. Love. We had dinner, and we sat and talked. Finally, Deacon Love said to me, "Reverend, did you get a letter from us?"

I said, "No, I didn't."

I believe the deacon was named brother Pugh.[9] Said, "Brother Pugh was supposed to have written you and notified you that the members had voted that your tenure was out, and that we had invited another man, a Reverend Jackson, to preach tomorrow."

Mrs. Love said, as she observed possibly this downcast look on my face—because the news shattered me—she said, "Young man, don't worry about that." Said, "If I were you, I wouldn't go to the church Sunday."

I said, "Well, I'll have to go. I don't have any way to get back home."

She said, "Well, God has many things in store for you."

I don't know whether she was aware of it, but she was very prophetic in that expression. So I was so downcast that I went on to my room, and I prayed, and I would lie down and think about it, and I would get up and pray again because I wasn't satisfied with the former prayer, and I would get back in bed, then I'd get up and pray again.

I eventually went to sleep, and got up and had breakfast and went to church. Most of the people were standing around on the outside because the invited guest preacher had not arrived.

After they'd stood for a long time outside, one or two of the deacons who were in sympathy with me—they were in sympathy with me as a young preacher, whether they wanted me as pastor or not—so they said, "Why don't we just go on and let Reverend Franklin preach for us since the other preacher's not here? And just carry on in the same manner that we've carried on with him the previous year?"

So they finally agreed upon it. I really wanted to preach that day as I had never preached before, because I wanted them to be sorry that they turned me off. So I preached, but I couldn't get too much above what I had been doing.

So I preached day and night, and the next morning I got the bus going back to Cleveland. But my bus was late, and when I got home, my father— I got home around nine o'clock that morning. Well, he'd been in the field since seven or seven-thirty, and he said, "Now this going off preaching and coming in this time of day is no good."

Said, "Now you have got to make up your mind whether you want to preach or plow."[10]

So I made up my mind that very day, and left home with virtually nothing. And I went down and talked with a blind friend of mine who was very active in our church, a very astute man named Jim. Jim said, "Well, son, you can stay here with me until you find you a place," and that's where I stayed till I got a little place in Cleveland.

I was preaching in and out of Cleveland for the next two years, sometimes at St. Peter's Rock, sometimes at rural churches in the area. I met my future wife at a church. A minister who pastored not far from her home in Shelby, Mississippi, Reverend Randall, invited me to his church. Not to preach; he just invited me there.

So I went out with him to his church, and Barbara, who later became my wife, was playing the piano for the church, and singing. Another local preacher who knew her personally, the late Reverend Honeywood, introduced me to her, and it started from there. I was still living in Cleveland, so I didn't have a chance to see her too much; I would go up to Shelby occasionally to see her.

I moved to Clarksdale to pastor some churches south of that town, and I would go back down to Shelby to see her, and I invited her to Clarksdale on one occasion, and eventually, about a year after I first met her, we got married. It was done in one of my member's homes. It was quite rainy that night, and there was no service scheduled. We had informed the people that we wanted to have the ceremony out there in one of my deacon's homes. And we had the preacher to come and meet us there; he performed the ceremony.

I stayed in Clarksdale for another year, pastoring in the rural area. I was pastoring a church by the name of Mount Olive, out from Shelby, and my wife was expecting when I went off to church. Her brother was going for the doctor, and of course it created a kind of anxiety. I had never had a child before, and it made me a little nervous and anxious. I was tremendously aware and conscious of how she was going to get along, you know. And I rushed back home from the church and the baby was here!

We moved to Greenville, Mississippi. The black Baptist Convention had provided a kind of seminary in Greenville, Greenville Industrial College. It was just a denominational school, seminary and trades to a limited extent. It was intended to develop into a great school, but at the time I went there it wasn't even accredited by the state.

They taught theology and regular literary subjects, and it did kind of challenge me to study. They had courses on preaching. The instructor would choose certain books, and he would lecture on them. He would require us either to orally recite what we had learned or to write it. Sometimes on Fridays one of the young preachers was called upon to give a message. He knew in advance that he was going to be called. It was all right for him to use notes as he spoke, but it was thought of as being better if he had become conversant with what he was going to talk about, to the point that he could just reel it off. This would communicate better; it would engage the audience to the point of getting them involved mentally with him.

The theologians at Greenville were Fundamentalists, and chose only conservative authors. They interpreted the Bible literally, saying things like man has been on the planet for 6000 years, stuff like that. They wouldn't dare touch upon anything that dealt with Darwin or evolution. I recall that they said that a sermon should have an introduction, a body, and a climax. The introduction would introduce what you wanted to talk about; in the body of the sermon you dealt with your theme; and your summary or climax would be a summary of all that you had been talking about before. You were supposed to choose a text on special occasions, like Mother's Day, fitting to the occasion.

I was thinking with some humor about a church that I had north of Shelby, on a plantation, Macedonia Baptist Church. I had been called to pastor at Greenville, to a much larger church, while I was going to school there. Once the Greenville church lost their minister, they invited me to come and preach, and afterwards they got together to determine whether it would be me or whether it would be some other preacher whom they invited. They always have that; they ask several preachers to come, and the people decide which one they want by majority vote.

Well, I felt that once I told the people at Macedonia that I was leaving that they would be terribly saddened. I happened to tell them before I preached, and instead of being saddened the reverse happened. They got mad. And there was absolutely no response to my sermon. It caught me unexpectedly.

In Greenville I had a place, rented a downstairs apartment, and I supported myself and paid my tuition wholly from preaching. In the meantime I had become friends with Dr. Perkins, the man that inspired me to preach. He invited me to come and preach for him in Clarksdale, where he was pastoring, and Memphis, where he was also pastoring. Eventually I had an invitation to come from Greenville and pastor two churches in Memphis. Dr. Perkins made no direct attempt to bring me to Memphis, but some of the members in Memphis possibly heard me at his church. I had one church out in the so-called Hollywood subdivision, and New Salem downtown.

Shortly after I got to Memphis I entered LeMoyne College. As a minister, it was possible to enter as a special student, and I went there for nearly three years. I had a general plan of subjects that were prescribed by the dean. Sociology, social sci it was called, and English literature, things like that. I recall studying about black people in the social sci course, but it didn't have the same kind of emphasis that it does now in departments of black studies. Then there wasn't any heavy emphasis on it, but they did teach about the equality of men irrespective of their races, and that differences came in only where background or environment or education were concerned.

My schedule was rather hectic. If I had two or three classes a day, I could usually be there about ten o'clock, and be ready to leave about one-thirty. Then I might visit hospitals or go by a sick member's house, things like that. Evenings I'd spend with my family, and studying.

One of the things I thought about when I was about to move to Memphis was that pastoring there would expand my mind, my experience, expose me to things that I had never been exposed to in Mississippi. When I got to Memphis, I met a variety of people. We had a ministers' alliance, where the preachers gathered every Tuesday, and one would review the Sunday school lesson for the other preachers, and another would preach. Some were inspiring, challenging; and some were not so inspiring, challenging. I remember one expressed opposition to a preacher saying *you* instead of *thou* without understanding that you and thou are synonyms, and that thou was an English expression; the Hebrew didn't say either. And this type of experience was rather educational to me in terms of cultivating me with biblical thinking beyond what I'd been exposed to in Mississippi.

I would characterize myself as a Fundamentalist prior to coming to

Memphis. But then I began to be exposed to new interpretations, and I started to go to LeMoyne, and I was exposed to new biblical views, and I started traveling, and came into contact with preachers around the country when I would go and run revivals and speak at ministers' conferences. And they would visit with me; usually several preachers daily. And we had discussions, both in the conferences and at the private home where I was stopping, or the hotel.

And my views and interpretations and understanding began to evolve. Of course this aroused within me some concern about my former views, but I regarded it more or less as a deepening. At that time my sermons may have begun to become more historically minded and less evangelical. Evangelism to me is simply stirring people up, to make them feel some spontaneous thing that may not be lasting, while if you preach to them in terms of the historical meaning it's altogether different. It has a more lasting effect because you're reaching their minds as well as their emotions.

In Mississippi I might have been more interested in reaching their emotions.[11] I was what they called a Spiritual preacher. That meant that if you preached in such a way with an intonation, and what you were saying had meaning for them and moved them, then you were a Spiritual preacher. But as I went along, I discovered that the emotional thing was short-lived. I saw people who would express those kinds of emotions yet were not changed at all. It's all right to do it; it's all right for one to express himself in that manner, shouting and all that. But I would like for him to have something mentally that would be lasting, because the mental can be spiritual, even more spiritual than the emotional.

My feeling about the Spirit and the preacher now is that the Spirit inspires you beyond what you have read, enlightens you, and gives you strength. But I do not feel when I preach that the Spirit is *controlling* what I am saying.

Most of the people that I lived around in Mississippi, with the exception of maybe one or two, never thought or talked about voting. They had what they called a *poll tax,* and if you went about to try to be registered as a voter, pay your poll tax, then your very life would be in danger. If you went up to answer the various questions in an attempt to qualify yourself, they would ask you kind of absurd, stupid questions about how many bubbles are in a bar of soap! (Laughs.) So blacks did not vote. Maybe one or two that the white people selected might vote. Not over two in a small community, small town like Cleveland.

The political situation was a bit more relaxed in Memphis. The whites usually selected their own man, their own black man, to represent blacks. The blacks would select those that they would permit to vote. The preachers were more or less religiously preoccupied, thinking about the world after. There were some who thought in terms of civil rights—the more advanced ones. But the average one was more or less indifferent, because of his condition.

You know, I think Doctor Benjamin Mays tells a story—he's Professor Emeritus at Morehouse College—about an alligator who was imported, I believe he said imported, from the Gulf; or he was brought from somewhere else, out of the country. And there was a fence built around the pool where they put him. He stayed in there quite a long while, for years. And then they removed the fence, but he never came out of that pool.

And I think some situations that whites imposed on blacks with respect to their political welfare so conditioned them that they became indifferent to voting and to their total political welfare. The white people had taught the preacher that politics had no place in the church, and that religion, in terms of society, was departmental. You're over here, this is over here, and this is taboo. And most of them were brought up with that kind of thinking.

I had my first radio broadcast in Memphis. I went to the station manager and talked about the possibility of a broadcast emanating from my church. The rates were considerably cheaper than they are here. So I got a weekly broadcast and it attracted people.

After I had been in Memphis about three years, a friend of mine passed who had a church in Memphis not too far from where I pastored. He was pastoring that church in Memphis and also Friendship Baptist Church in Buffalo, New York. He died. And I was asked by his membership to preach the funeral. I preached the funeral, and the people who were accompanying his body from Buffalo were impressed by my sermon and invited me to come to Buffalo. I went up there and preached, and they eventually elected me as their new pastor.

But before I left Memphis, I came back one Sunday for a baptismal service, and I had on a kind of a Prince Albert outfit that the church had given me in Buffalo. Tails and all that. And we'd had the baptismal service out in the backyard of the church, the pool was in the back, and people were crowded and all, and after the baptism I went over to put on my new suit that Friendship Church had given me.

And while I was in there dressing, just as I was finishing, I heard a mighty scramble next door, at the church. And I went out the back door, and just as I went out the back door of the house next door, a man was running down the back steps, with his handkerchief up to his neck. Someone had cut him. A man had cut him.

Well, it turned out that I had an usher who was so-called morally loose. And she was going with two guys on the usher board. One was

Anderson, the other one was Pugh. Pugh was a very quiet man, very seldom talked. If you asked him something, he would answer you in as few words as he could. He said to this girl, "I don't want to see you with Anderson."

And to talk to this woman in that manner would be like talking to the wind. Not only did he see her with him again, she came to church with him! He was standing at the entrance of the church, the front door. She sat right down on the seat in front of him.

He lived about a block from the church; he walked out without saying anything, went home, got his knife, came back, and ripped her neck open. I don't see how she lived. And when he ripped her neck, then he reached for the other guy, but Anderson was moving so fast he just busted the skin on his neck.

So Anderson was coming out of the church as I was coming out the back door of the house, and he ran between the house and the church. Someone had called an ambulance, and the ambulance had not gotten there for the moment. He went over and hid. He knew that someone had called it and went over and hid, and when the ambulance came, and they opened up the ambulance door, (laughs) he ran all the way up to the driver's seat!

When I went up to the front between the house and the church, this girl, they were bringing her out, and the blood was hot, in the summertime, just leaping like that, all down her legs to her feet. And she lived. She lived. I really don't see how. I was looking into her neck.

Pugh ran, and some of the officers followed him running, and he got under a house, up in the next block. There was one guy that was there helping to flush him out who was just a little off, you know (laughs). And he said, "Come on out from under there. You messed up us church today! You come out from under there!" (Laughs.)

And he would start under the house where the man was, and Pugh would come out with this knife. And this guy turned around, went back, and got a brick, and pointed it at his head (laughs) and zoomed that brick under the house.

It hit this guy right on the head and he fell out. And he hollered, "I'll come out! I'll come out!"

"Come on out, then. You messed up us church today!"

I drove to Buffalo from Memphis; I had a car, a Buick, and I drove. My wife and I drove. We left the children[12] with her mother for a few weeks, and we went back and got the children. In Buffalo there was not so much overt segregation as down South. But it was subtle. It was there in terms of jobs: where one could work or could not work. Or in the political situation. But eating facilities were integrated, and my children went to mixed schools.

Moving to Buffalo didn't give me the chance to graduate from LeMoyne. As a special student I entered the University of Buffalo for one semester. I studied mostly literature, American, and some English literature, too. I felt it would widen the horizon of my understanding.

Were black writers taught?

I think only Richard Wright. *Native Son,* and his other book that came out at the time I was there—*Black Boy.* They incorporated that into it.

In Buffalo I thought that my position was improved. The congregation made more money and they could respond to the church financially better than the people of Memphis could. They had greater job security. It wasn't quite as large as New Bethel here in Detroit, but it was considered a large church and it had a large membership. And they were comparable to New Bethel in giving. They had a very good choir, too.

Many of the people in my congregation worked for Bethlehem Steel, automobile factories, other plants. Most of them were Southerners who had moved to Buffalo looking for better living conditions. The people were very nice, very responsive to me. I was paid a regular salary along with my house and its maintenance. But for a Southerner like me it was too cold, too much snow, too damp, all that kind of thing.

I didn't like preaching in Buffalo because of the conservative, staid, frontier type of life there. I wanted to be in a more fluid situation. By that I mean that I wanted to be in a city where there were crossroads of transportation. Trains, buses, planes, where people are coming and going, conventions of all kinds, and migrations.

I wanted a city not static in its growth. People weren't coming in and out of Buffalo as they would Detroit or Chicago or New York. So I felt that my chances would be greater in a more fluid situation. Maybe my reasoning was not altogether logical. I just felt that way. I felt kind of cut off from the onflow of life in this country.

I preached at the National Baptist Convention in Detroit in 1945. Detroit had a reputation as a city of good preachers; cities get those sorts of reputations. New Bethel had a pastor then, but eventually there was a disruption in the church, and the church split. He took a group somewhere else and this portion of New Bethel stayed there. They sent me a telegram and asked me to come on a certain Sunday and preach for them then, which I did. And then I went back to Buffalo.

New Bethel had a meeting in the next couple of weeks and they elected me as the pastor. There had been other pastors coming in and out, but they settled on me, and they informed me that they would expect me the first Sunday in June, 1946. And I was there.

The people at Friendship expressed surprise and resentment. They talked to me. They wanted to know what was it that I was seeking—a better salary? Or was I dissatisfied with the church? I told them no, it wasn't that. I just felt that it was a step forward to go to Detroit.

I came to New Bethel when it was in a dilapidated building that had been converted from a bowling alley. It was kind of a storefront, on Hastings Street. Comparatively old. And I wasn't satisfied with the building, though I liked the congregation.

So they had about twenty-five or thirty thousand dollars on hand for a new building, a new church, and as we went along for the next few years we constantly added to that. Raising money in church is an art; obligations are so heavy. Here, now, the mortgage is $1717 a month; and the upkeep of the church, the maintenance, salaries for custodians, pastor, secretaries, utilities, is even more than that per month.

Before I was the pastor I was invited to come here and preach, and I was just sitting and looking at the crowd. And they were passing the plates. And the offering was something like forty or forty-five dollars with about five or six hundred people there! (Laughs.) I made a decision that if I became pastor I would change that, and I did.

In Memphis and Buffalo I had people get up out of their seats and come to the front of the church,[13] and we do it that way now. There's a psychological reason for doing it; in black churches you get more that way.

It is said that on one occasion a minister preached a great sermon. It so happened that his offering came after the sermon instead of before. And he preached, and people were impressed, and there was a man in the audience who hadn't been to church for many years, if ever. And he was so impressed until he decided that he was going to give a hundred dollars. But then as the fervor subsided he was looking at the ushers, who had started at the back of the church, going down the benches, passing the plate up and down, and moving toward the front. He was somewhere near the front, and of course he was watching what other people were giving.

And he decided, he said, "Well, nobody else is giving that amount, so I'll give fifty." Well, as they got closer to his bench, he decided, "I'll give twenty-five." The fervor was continually subsiding. And he said, "Instead of twenty-five, I think I'll give ten." And it is said that by the time they got to him (laughs) he stole five dollars off the plate!

So when you get them up to the table, they're not likely to do that. Not only that, but they will give more because of the people that are standing there. The minister's looking down and they'll give more.

But shortly after I had come to New Bethel, the officers of the church said they knew a black insurance man who himself was a preacher. And he told the officers verbally that with what we had—if we would exhaust those funds—he would step in and carry the building to its completion.

I didn't like it, and I got a committee and went to him. Set down and said, "I think we need a bit more than just an oral agreement. I think we ought to have something that's binding from our side and you."

He said, "No, no, I can't do that, because if you tear the building down, you don't have any collateral." And he went through this kind of thing.

The officers had blind confidence. They insisted. I'm a new preacher, so I go along. The insurance man kept saying, "All you've got to do is get the building up, get the roof on, get the windows framed, get the doors framed, and we'll come in."

Well, the officers were very enthusiastic about that because they knew this man, and blah blah blah. We tore the old place down and we built on the same spot, on Hastings Street. We got the building up, we got the roof on, we got the windows framed, we got the doors framed. He didn't come through.

So we were outdoors a little over two years. We were meeting at different church buildings in the area, in the afternoon. We eventually got one of the city's recreational buildings, called Brewster Center, and we were meeting there on Sunday mornings, but we could not meet there on Sunday nights.

So on this particular Sunday night I went down to the Gotham Hotel on John R, across from the Medical Center, to have dinner. And the real-estate man who sold me this house saw me and he came over to my table and sat. In the course of just exchanging pleasantries, he said, "Look, have you observed this man here on Woodward back of the hotel? Lofton?"

I said, "Yes, I know Reverend Lofton quite well."

He said, "You know what his thing is." Said, "You know, he has a great crowd, and he whispers numbers to people. Or at least he says, 'I saw shoes,' or 'I saw hats,' you know, and many of the people hit."

He said, "Now if you would go into that kind of thing, I would go into it with you. And tonight instead of you being outdoors, and sitting here in the Gotham with no church, nowhere to have services tonight, you could be in Europe, with five cars at home!"

I listened to his discussion, and I said, "Well, I don't believe in any form of gambling in the church. And once I come to that point, I'm just going to quit the church and go to gambling!"[14]

And that was that. You know, the building that we now have was once occupied by Prophet Jones. The Oriole Theater. He had a group of people who followed him superstitiously. His appeal was mystical. People felt that he could tell them things about their future, possibly touch them and bless them in terms of health or in terms of prosperity. And of course there were suggestions in his talk about good numbers to play,[15] stuff like that.

Some of the members drifted away, and I started running around trying to get a broadcast. I had had a broadcast in Memphis, and I had one in

Buffalo. I knew reaching the whole city was much better than just preaching to the people who just came into the church. But while we were out of our building, and we were out for nearly three years, it was very difficult to establish a broadcast.

Eventually I got that broadcast. The agent said to me, "The only thing I have right now is a station in Dearborn." He said, "It doesn't come through quite as clear as I'm sure you would like or as I would like, but if you are with us, the first opening that comes, you'll have the benefit of getting it."

So we hung in there for a few weeks, and after a few weeks we ran a deficit of about nine hundred dollars. And the officers were disturbed; there was constant grumbling and complaining, and they projected their complaints to the members.

So I had a meeting and told them, "I'll tell you what. You just turn Sunday night over to me. I will liquidate the indebtedness, and the church will be relieved of any responsibility for this deficit, or any responsibility involving the broadcast." And that same, no, the following week, the man called me and gave me an hour over WJLB where we are now. That was about 1952; late in 1951 we were coming from Dearborn. So I started preaching on the radio, and the people seemed as it were to come up out of the ground.

We liquidated that indebtedness, we assumed responsibility for the ongoing of the broadcast financially, and then they began to grumble again (laughs) because any monies above the expenses became mine—because they had given the total thing over to me to duck the responsibility of liquidating that indebtedness. So they started grumbling again!

It didn't move me at all. I continued right on. "And now there's one other way that we can have the broadcast," I said. "We come on at ten," I said; "I'll be here at eight and have the regular service then. You run the broadcast, you be responsible." So they didn't want that.[16] So it continues that way now.

I thought about a man who used to teach me theology[17] when he was in the city. And he said to me on one occasion, "Reverend, you don't realize that people turn their radio on to hear you preach. All that singing is not necessary." He said, "The people want to hear you. They should have one song, and then the sermon."

I said to him, "Then I wouldn't have a choir. People are imbued with the instinct or the desire for recognition, recognition in terms of participation. And your program must provide that if you want them to attend regularly. You must give them a place in the program."

And it was in the back of my mind when he said that, that I see now why he didn't have a church, because he didn't know how to involve people. One of the great psychological needs is recognition.

We eventually had a high-interest loan and finished rebuilding on Hastings Street. After the broadcast started, the congregation grew tremendously.[18] People would line up outside the church ahead of time to get in for the broadcast on Sunday nights. Some nights they would have to get there an hour before service started.

Our building was torn down with the urban renewal program in 1960. We got a hundred and some odd thousand for it, and we moved to a theater on Twelfth Street—Rose Park Boulevard, now—and we stayed there about two years. In the meantime we bought this building where we are now,[19] and we renovated it at about three hundred and fifty thousand. We got a bank loan from the Michigan National Bank, and carried it right on.

There has been a little falling off[20] since we moved to this section of the city in 1963. However, it seems that we have arrived at a more disciplined and dedicated membership, where we raise as much or more with those that we have now, as opposed to the standing crowds around Hastings.

I've never had problems with people telling me what to preach, but I've had problems with people. When I first came here, there was a man that more or less controlled the church. And as I gradually began to gain control, this upset him, and I had a little problem with him. He left, after I turned him out. He had three or four other guys with him, but they didn't split the church. He was a trustee.

How do you turn out a trustee?

By the vote of the people, your influence with the people. What you do is let it be established that he's in opposition to the leader of the church, the pastor. Let it be established; don't jump on him prematurely. Wait until people come to you and say, "This man's fighting you wherever he has a chance to." And then you begin to act on it. Talk to all of them. There's not too much that you have to say, because they know about it.

We had no difficulties in adjusting to our new surroundings in Detroit. Neither did our children, or not to my knowledge. They seemed to have fallen right in. We knew a few people prior to our coming here, and a lot of people at the church. My wife played for one of the choirs, directed it. Piano; she had done that before she left Memphis.

People loved her. We weren't too involved with them socially; we were involved with them in terms of the church program. She got along beautifully, beautifully. She had no problem. To me, people who respect the minister's wife and encourage her, admire her for what she is doing, like to hear her sing—I don't see why she has any difficulty, although I have often heard it said that it is difficult to be a minister's wife.

I think she only has difficulties when she goes in and tries to compete with the established leaders there. That might bring about conflict, but she never had any problem like that. The women in the church would call and talk to her. But in their different meetings, very seldom she went to those. She would go out to rehearsals and come back home, and in her choir they loved and admired her.

In 1952 my wife died.[21] Afterwards I went on a trip to the Baptist World Alliance in London. But the Holy Land was something I wanted to see and experience, so I went there as a tourist. It so happened that Clara Ward[22] was along, also as a tourist. Jerusalem was the ultimate end of the trip, but I had gone to London, and to Paris, to Rome, and to Athens and Cairo, to Lebanon, and to Syria. I had noted in Egypt that some of the women had the regular Eastern style mode of dress, with the veil and all, or half-veil. But when we got to Syria, Damascus, I never saw a woman's face; all of them were veiled. I was told that they could see you but you couldn't see them. I wondered about the type of material. I wondered what social situation, what cultural situation would render these people to feel that it was necessary to completely cover a woman's face?

We got a guide to drive us from Damascus to Jerusalem; this was about 150 miles. And the Arab driver was a speedster on these narrow roads in Palestine. Sometimes we'd be driving along a narrow road and there was a deep incline right off the road, and he would go around a curve, and it was one of the most frightening experiences I had ever had.

I was also astounded when I saw the river Jordan, near Jerusalem. I was thinking of the river Jordan in terms of how the river had been celebrated in song and poetry and prose, and I was looking for a river something comparable to the Mississippi River, or the Ohio River. And here was a little narrow stream which they called a river, and it was astounding to me. (Laughs.)

It was amazing also to walk around in Jerusalem and observe the sights, the historical sights. The two Calvaries—the Catholic and Protestant versions historically—and I noticed the Arabs were selling meat along the streets, with the sheds, toppings, over the streets, and the meat just lying out there raw, and the flies, the donkeys walking up and down the streets and leaving their droppings on the streets.

Of course in Israel it was altogether a different situation when it comes to sanitary conditions, as modern as Detroit. As we left Jerusalem, going up to Haifa, coming back to Tel Aviv, from which point we left for the States, I saw over the ancient soil, the parched hillsides, that the Jews had vast sprinkling systems that covered whole fields, and man-made forests, and man-made lakes. It was most interesting. Most interesting.

I had been curious about recording, and when I came back to the States I talked to some people in the industry. I was pastoring the church at

that time down on Hastings, near the periphery of the city. There was a girl—
she played for the young folks' choir—named Winona Carr; she turned to be
an entertainer later. And somebody from one of the record labels, that was
interested in her, came. And I talked with him, but he wasn't interested in
me.

One night I was preaching on the air, and a guy down the street,
who's dead, a black man named Joe Battles,[23] he was coming from Inkster[24]
and was listening. And he came on to the church, and after the dismissal he
came up to me and said, "Man, the way these people come out here to hear
you and listen to you, if you would record this, people would buy it." Said,
"Why don't you let me tape your sermons? I have a little rapport with Chess
Recording Company. I know the man, I knew him when he got started, and
I helped him a great deal. I'm sure that he would consider it."

I didn't think too much of it right then. I said, "We'll get together
and sit down and go over the idea and see what we can come up with."

So a few days later we talked. He went about it, taped the sermons,
went to Chicago, contacted Chess, and came back with a contract. I signed,
he managed, and, of course, the thing mushroomed.

That was about 1953. I had thought of it in terms of recording on the
spot, live at the church, right out of a regular service, and the record sales
more or less for people to hear them. I didn't know that they would respond
the way that they did. There is a radio station in Nashville, Tennessee,[25] which
has a kind of nationwide radius. One of the main sponsors was Randy's Record
Shop. They sold my records all over the country. Well, people started hearing
them, and they wanted to see me in their local cities. And Mrs. Ward[26]
immediately seized the opportunity to conscript me to come in and work with
her.

It so happened that the National Baptist Convention was meeting in
Memphis, and my first engagement was after the convention. I was to meet
the Ward Singers in Houston, Texas. Mrs. Ward—Clara's mother—asked me
if I would come from Memphis, from the convention, the Sunday during the
convention, the day it ended, and come and preach on her program at the city
auditorium with the Ward Singers. I said, "Yes."

Mrs. Ward was quite experienced in the field. She'd been out there
a long time, and she knew all the ins and outs of the trade. It was a new thing
for me. She said, "I can't give you but $500."

I said, "Okay, that's all right. I'll be off anyway. I have no obligations
that Sunday; if I were not with you I would be at the convention."

So I went in there that Saturday evening, and I checked in at the
hotel, and I talked to some people that I knew, some preachers that I knew.
And one of them, who was a deejay and had been involved in the promotion
of the program, said to me, "Reverend, I know you're getting a bundle on this

program. The Ward Singers have never been to the city auditorium before. They've usually been singing here in the high school auditorium, and that was it. But to go the city auditorium! Those people are coming there to hear you, because we've been really burning up your records down here."

I didn't say anything about it, but after talking to him a good while it began to go through my mind, were these people using me? So the next morning at the hotel there were several black girls who were maids, and I wasn't supposed to be at the auditorium until three-thirty, and they were knocking on the door. And I asked who was it.

Said, "It's the maid."

I said, "Well, I'm not dressed yet."

She said, "Well, when you get dressed would you let us know?" Said, "All of the maids would like to see you; we've been hearing your sermons."

So I said, "Yes," and when I got dressed I opened the door, and they came in, and shook my hand, expressed happiness to have a chance to talk to me and see me. And I said to myself, "Now this thing here, if all of this interest has been generated in this town on the program because I'm on it, I'd better go down to the auditorium. I know Mrs. Ward is down there."

So I went down, and when I got there, about one-thirty, the place was jammed. I found Mrs. Ward and the promoter. I said, "Mrs. Ward, I understand this is your first time being at the auditorium."

"Yes, it is."

"I see. Well, do you want to up that agreement because of the success of the program?"

"Well, you know, I don't have anything to say about that, Reverend. I, it's the promoter, what the promoter told me."

But I knew that wasn't true. I knew Mrs. Ward. Nobody deals with Mrs. Ward on that basis. So I said, "Well, let's talk with him, and we'll talk."

So the promoter had become a little hostile when he found I wanted more. I said, "I want fifteen hundred dollars."

He said, "Now don't get big-eyed!" (Laughs.) "You want to take it all!"

I said, "Do you mean to tell me at two-fifty and three-fifty with about six thousand people here, that fifteen hundred dollars is taking it all?" I said, "It seems to me it's the other way round. You want to take it all!" (Laughs.)

I went in my inside coat pocket and got my plane ticket from Detroit to Memphis to Houston to Detroit. I said, "Now this ticket has already been paid for. Now I either get the fifteen hundred or you-all take care of the program and I'll be glad to go home today, this day!" (Laughs.) They gave me the fifteen hundred.

What led you to go on tour with the Ward Singers?

Primarily it was the responsibility of educating the children. In a low-income congregation when they are paying you as a pastor, they resent the fact that you are calling upon them—in addition to what they are paying you—to help you educate your children. Because many of them have children for whom they are making no effort to educate, they resent you asking them to help you educate your own. Mainly because they have a kind of a low-level appreciation for education itself. So the need for getting them through school motivated me to go out and try to make the necessary monies to finance their education.

We started that way. The singers—and in most cases there were other singers than the Ward Singers, sometimes the Davises or sometimes the Dixie Hummingbirds,[27] other groups—they would sing first, and then I would come on and close the thing with a sermon. This took place in city auditoriums, schools, or churches. And they at the time would guarantee me a certain amount, six or seven hundred dollars on this date, five or six at another date, depending on the size of the city and the expected draw. Many times it paid off, many times it didn't. With the entourage I had, I had to pay these drivers, singers, musicians, hotel, transportation. Sometimes we'd come out and sometimes we wouldn't.

Did you think it somewhat unusual to be doing what you were doing?

Yes, it was unusual to me at first. It was unusual because no other preacher at the time had acquired that status in terms of recordings. I considered it a challenge. It was different from the traditional evangelistic thing, revivals. The fact that people were hearing me and demanding to see me and to hear me preach in person, all that kind of thing, it became a challenge.

Soon I went on my own, with my own entourage rather than the Wards. My daughter Aretha started touring with me as a solo singer at about the age of fifteen. Some of them were long tours. For example, sometimes if I flew to Richmond, and preached there on Sunday afternoon, I might preach Monday night somewhere else, maybe in North Carolina, and maybe the next Wednesday night I would preach at some other point, maybe Raleigh, and Friday night in Durham. Then I would fly home to preach on Sunday at New Bethel, and the next week early possibly meet my driver and the singers in Atlanta. I would have my car on the road with the driver, two singers, and a pianist, and I covered their hotel bills and transportation, and my plane backward and forward from home to where they were.

I continued this kind of schedule from the latter part of '53 until the early '60s. I think it kind of broke me down. It was too much, because you had the responsibility, the total responsibility. And people expect a lot out of the black preacher. Many of them feel that unless you extend yourself and expend a lot of energy you haven't done anything. So when one sees himself failing in health, as I did, it is a major concern. After the early '60s I gradually slowed down my tours and concentrated on New Bethel. Altogether I must have toured for fourteen or fifteen years, and all the while being pastor of New Bethel.

Can you describe a typical stop on one of these tours?

Suppose my group had to drive from here to Atlanta. There had been previous arrangements as to where they would stop, and they would do as most people would do, travel, stop and eat, and move on, with the driver steadily driving, stopping when necessary. Say they got in this morning early—and in the early afternoon I would fly there. And it may be necessary that we have some personal appearances on the radio. Either the promoter was a deejay, or he had certain deejays that he wanted you to appear on their shows, to enhance the program, which might be that night or the next day.

The deejay would ask, "Reverend Franklin, how is New Bethel?"

"Reverend Franklin, how do you like Atlanta? People are waiting to see you tomorrow. I know many of your fans are listening."

"Reverend Franklin, where do you go from here?"

They might ask you something else; they might come up with something humorous. Then I would go back to the hotel and try to get some rest, but you have got to kind of ride herd on your people, because they are kind of indifferent. They're not worried about being punctual or making time, so you've really got to stay right on them to get them on the show.

Did you make your entrance after the singing was over or did you usually wait on stage throughout the whole program?

I was on the stage,[28] because in that type of thing it's not typically show business. People want to see you. They don't want to have to say, "Where is he?" And you can't charge the same thing in a religious program, because you are dealing with people who are religiously oriented. Maybe they may not be very good church members, but they are religiously oriented, hence they will come to an extra thing like that. So you can't charge them five-fifty, six-fifty, and ten dollars. You have to charge just a few dollars at the door. You couldn't depend on a collection. You wouldn't even get your expenses.

I would preach whatever the deejay had been playing,[29] and what was indicated to the deejay that the people liked most. At first I resented these requests. I had the attitude that I would have at the church, that people should be ready to listen to whatever I chose to preach on, but people are not like that. They want to hear what they have been hearing. Now you may have a better sermon on something else in your own judgment, but as far as they're concerned, they don't want to hear it.

You're always hopeful that you can move them, inasmuch as they've invited you there, and they come out with certain expectations of the situation, and you're hopeful that you can move them in more ways than just the emotional thing—that you can impart some thoughtfulness and inspiration in them.

They usually responded strongly. Some people shouted and some people hollered at me, waved their hands, all that, stand up and point at you (laughs). It gave me a thrill to see people react that way, because I felt that in some way it was helpful to them, if nothing more than to raise their spirits. At the close I offered an invitation, and if anybody wanted to join any of the churches in that city we would send them to those churches. Many times the pastor of a particular church that a person came forward wanting to join was already there. It was generally understood that anybody was free to attend; it was not advertised as a denominational thing. We got quite a few white people to attend, but it was predominantly black.

I led a march here in Detroit in 1963. It was as big as the March on Washington. We held it in Cobo Hall. The chief of police was on the stage, and he said to us that there were two hundred thousand people in the streets. And of course the papers played it down to a hundred and twenty-five thousand. But the police chief was constantly in touch with the policemen in the streets, and he said publicly there were two hundred thousand. The idea grew out of the thrust of civil rights at the time. We got in touch with Dr. King, and he agreed, and came, and spoke, just like he did in Washington. He used the same speech, as a matter of fact, *I Have a Dream*.

I had gone down to Memphis in 1968 prior to his assassination. He had a rally scheduled, and he had invited me to come and preach. He had some people in Memphis training people for what he really wanted—how they were supposed to conduct themselves, and the whole layout; and how they were going to march from a Methodist church, Hernando to Beale Street, out Beale Street to Main Street, and then up Main Street. And some of the people who had not had this training, when they saw all of these people marching down the street, they jumped in the march, undisciplined.

I was in town. I had come in that morning around three o'clock, stopping at the Rivermont, the headquarters of the Holiday Inn. He was stopping there. And I told him, "Well, I'm getting in a bit too late to join your march, but tonight I'll be there."

But they had looting going out Beale Street. Some of the fellows started breaking into pawnshops, clothing stores, and they had to cancel the rally. About two or three weeks later he went back, and he was killed. It was a tragic experience, shattering to me.

Did you think Ray did it alone or do you think there was a conspiracy?

I believe there was a conspiracy. I really do. One young man who was very close to Dr. King, James Bevoe, went to Memphis and gained audience with Ray, talked to him for two hours. The police let him go in and sit down and talk. This guy was working on his Ph.D., a very clever young man. And he said, "There's no way—the mentality of that man?—there's no way that he could have gotten out of Memphis, and gone to Atlanta, and gotten out of the country into Canada, and on to England, without some help."

Dr. King sat right in my basement one Sunday night. He had spoken for my Men's Day, and he said, "Frank," he said, "I will never live to see forty." He said, "Some of our white brothers are very, very sick, and they are dangerous. I'll never see forty." And he was thirty-nine when he was killed.

I'm less active in civil rights now, but I have the same type of thinking as I did then. Of course I was a part of SCLC, and later PUSH, Jesse Jackson's thing. We embraced the nonviolent philosophy. I was active then; I went more than I do now. I preached at the Poor People's March in Washington.

I preached in Washington for Jesse Jackson one night, and he had a young man there that was one of his secretaries, a smart, young white guy. And he was small, much smaller than you are. And the police in Washington, they had some kind of small riot, some disturbance. It wasn't a big thing, but the police at first said that we would have to cancel the service.

Some of the leaders went to them, talked to them and said, "Now *we* are not rioting. If you hadn't told us, we wouldn't even know there was a riot. And we are peacefully going on with this civil rights thing."

So they finally consented for us to go on, but the police were going about to get most of the people off the streets. And Jesse said to this boy— they knew one another quite well—he said, "You better get your little white self in this car before some of these black folk kill you!" (Laughs.)

In Detroit there was a movement called the New Republic of Africa. I had no affiliation with that particular group. But they rented the church, and it was on a Saturday night. Nineteen sixty-eight sometime. The only member of our church that was there was the janitor. And of course about twelve o'clock, Ben Washington[30] called me and told me, "Reverend, Reverend, you'd better get up and come down here. There's been shooting down here!"

And I said, "Shooting?"

Said, "You know that movement that rented the church? They had some kind of shooting with the police!"

Well, the police apparently had had them under surveillance for quite some time before, and they were circulating in the community, around the church. And they had guards, armed guards, for the officials of this movement. These guys had on fatigue boots, and uniforms, and something like berets, and they had these rifles on their shoulders.

So when I got down there, I went into the church, went into the lobby, and attempted to go into the sanctuary. The head policeman, the one that was apparently in charge, said, "You can't go in."

I said, "Why? There's no shooting. Nobody's in there."

"Well, they're cleaning up now."

The police, what they were really doing, they were gathering the bullets that had lodged in the benches. Nobody was hurt, fortunately, in there. What precipitated the whole thing was that these movement officials were getting into their cars, with their guards standing by, and when the police got out of their cars with their guns, these guys just started shooting, outside.

The people were still in the church. Just the officials were coming out. And they shot a policeman. The other policeman that was in the car with the one that got shot called for help, and they were right there within about a minute and a half, right at the church. And they came in shooting.

Someone called out, "Get on the floor! Get on the floor!" And they were shooting all through there. The pulpit desk had several holes in it.

They said there was a shootout, but there was really no shootout. Most of the glass was inside the lobby, and, as I showed the police commissioner, in the back pews—the pews near the entrance into the auditorium—the splinters were lying in the seats. There were no splinters back of the benches—which meant that the shooting was coming inside rather than coming outside. The policemen were doing the shooting. There wasn't any physical sign of any shots going out of the church. But, you know, the police are going to respond when that policeman got shot. And that was outside.

I went upstairs to the office, and (laughs) Shelby[31] was sitting there fanning: "Ooh my God, ooh Lawd, who let those people have the church? Ooh my God, they torn up our church!"

I said, "Shelby, we are in the throes of a revolution, a social revolution. Some people have lost their lives in this revolution, and we have lost a little glass. I think we got out cheap."

What ever happened to the movement?

I don't know. Haven't heard too much from it since then. The police put some of the leaders in jail. This seemed to abort it, you know.

In Mississippi the black minister was extremely limited in his participation in the political situation. The power structure was totally dominated by whites. Now, while it is predominantly white, blacks have moved into it to a limited degree. In the old days if I wanted to buy a church building there to start up a church I would have to get some white person to intercede between me and the bank, if I got it at all.

In Buffalo, or Detroit, or Chicago, or Los Angeles, the minister is involved. He helps his congregation in terms of presenting before them different candidates, and recommending. He leaves them free, of course, to choose; but he recommends certain people. Representative Conyers[32] courted us when he was running. He was there every Sunday night and wanted to help make the announcements on the broadcasts. And the minister is interested in what the Board of Education is doing, if the classrooms are too crowded, things like that. He's involved in the total structure.

In a rural situation the pastor's duties are negligible. The rural people do not make as many demands upon you, for your time, because the minister doesn't live at the place where he's pastoring. If he had four churches, a church for each Sunday, he lives possibly in Clarksdale, for example—I was living in Clarksdale and I was pastoring south of Clarksdale in four of the little towns. You are not as available to the congregation or to the respective congregations as you might be if you were living in the area. Of course if somebody is seriously ill, they will try to get in touch with you and ask you to come; or if someone passes, come and take you up a funeral, and go back.

In a situation such as I live in now, or in Memphis, or in Buffalo, you're right there, people know your number, and they're constantly calling on you: "My son is in jail"; or "I need a lawyer"; or "I want you to go to court and talk to the judge concerning my son"—things like that. Or "I want you to come by the hospital," or somebody in a rest home.

A man that's farming thinks a little differently from a man that's working in a plant or a man that's running a business or a teacher or a doctor. But I think the needs of the people are essentially the same. There are some needs that a more mature and trained person will handle himself, where the rural people are more or less reliant on the pastor for guidance. The people here in Detroit seek some guidance, but not in menial things; they handle those themselves.

Nowadays I wake up more or less with the telephone. People are calling about various things. Unfortunately the members don't understand that. They think only in terms of them having called, but the variety of calls that you get about a variety of different things never occurs to most of them— maybe a few—but not to most of them.

So I wake up with a phone call. And the phone call is about somebody got sick, somebody has passed, or somebody wants the use of the church, somebody wants me to preach on this pastor's anniversary, somebody wants me to come to the hospital to see him, or somebody wants to talk to me about some problem that they're having. That's a typical day. I get out of bed, cook my own breakfast sometimes. Bacon and eggs, sausage, toast, milk, coffee. After breakfast I go back up and start talking on the phone again about various things, to various people. Might be on the phone for hours. Maybe it's eleven o'clock before I eat breakfast; and lunch, I'm not hungry at that time. And the phone doesn't stop ringing.

In the afternoon I'll maybe go over to the church, or go somewhere else, go downtown, maybe go to the hospital. Go in, visit with them, sit and talk with them, and if they ask me to pray, I pray, out loud, a quiet prayer but in audible words.

I remember I was in the Harper Hospital once. On my broadcast, and on other religious radio broadcasts, they were expressing sympathy and prayer for me. And a Pentecostal woman preacher and her husband—both of them were preachers—came and I was lying in bed and they just walked in and said, "Elder Franklin"[33]—they didn't use the word *Reverend*—"my husband and I want to pray for you." And they were talking loud.

I said, "No. No. I'm desirous of you praying for me, but you can do that at home." I didn't want them disturbing the other patients by their hollering and going on.

So they got a little vexed by it, the woman did. "You don't want prayer?"

"Yes, I want prayer, but it doesn't necessarily have to be here."

So whenever I go to pray for people I just give a quiet prayer. It could be disturbing to other patients.

I believe in healing; naturally, if I believe in the Bible I believe in it, but I don't believe in the demonstrative type of thing, where you come and kneel here, and you come and kneel there, and I'm going to lay my hands on you, and this, that, and the other. I never presumed that I had special powers in healing. People come to me and ask me to pray for them, but the demonstrative healing is a little outside the Baptist tradition.

After a hospital visit I might go to another hospital or I might come home, or I might stop by the church, get my mail, find out who has been calling, what the general situation is. A secretary is there every day, except Wednesday. For example, this morning a woman called to tell me she wanted me to come to a meeting Thursday night of next week, with the young people's choir, to plan for the quarterly Youth Day program.

Then I might come back home and cook supper if I'm hungry. I like fish, chicken, pork, but I don't eat much pork now because of my blood pressure. And there are more phone calls in the evening. For example, a young woman called me from New York yesterday. She used to have people here and she would come visit them from New York and come to the church frequently. And she said that her daughter had entered into the practice of prostitution. And I know that she has had a lot of trouble with her. And it was rather unusual because the family is a very nice family, from West Virginia. And the grandfather of the girl who was in prostitution was also a preacher. The mother said she got out six hundred and some dollars to get her daughter out for Mother's Day. And two or three weeks before, four hundred and something; and a few weeks before then, three something. She said that it was done just for her own satisfaction. She didn't feel that this would do anything to change her, but she just wanted to do it.

At night I study and meditate. I read last night on this thing I might preach Sunday morning—the man at the pool in Jerusalem. Jesus said, "Do you want to be made whole?" That's an interesting question, isn't it? Obviously to some degree he had wanted to be or he wouldn't have lain there for thirty-eight years. That's an interesting question. "Do you *want* to be?"

In the early 1960s my children Cecil and Erma were finishing high school. And of course I had some plans for them. I made arrangements for Cecil at Morehouse and for Erma at Morris Brown, in Atlanta. And I had a little difficulty with Cecil about going to school. When he finished high school, he didn't want to go to college.

I wanted him to go to a southern college, black college, because I felt that he could get a new perspective on himself and black people in that circumstance. It seems to me that in the northern and eastern and southwestern and middle western cities, the so-called underworld people have captured the imagination of young people with their mink coats and Cadillac cars and nice homes. These things can muddle the imagination of young people and render them completely lost of any sense of values.

And so in the southern cities, for the most part, the societal situation is structured a little differently. It seems that the lawyers, the doctors, the teachers, the businessmen are at the top of the social structure, and they are looked up to much more than they are in the cities in other parts of the country.

Cecil said, "Daddy, I don't want to go to college."

I said, "Well, I've made all the arrangements. I have you a place right off campus, and your tuition has been paid, and I'm going to take you to the airport and put you on the plane.

"Now when you get to Atlanta, if you have decided that you don't want to go to school, then just remember: don't come back here, because my plans for you as long as you are here are for you to go to school. Now if you feel that you can assume the responsibilities for yourself, well and good. You don't have to come back. You don't have to go to school." So he went, and it worked out fine.

Predestination is not a part of my preaching. I cannot believe that God has, for example, predestined that a train would run over you, and then see him as a loving God. What father would plan for the destruction of his son? That would be a contradiction in the character of God to me.

Some people even now think they should do good because they are afraid God will take vengeance upon them if they do differently. But I don't think that one should embrace God in terms of fear. I think one should embrace God in terms of love. I believe that God is love, and that God is a father, and we are pictured as his children. Thus I cannot think of God being a father and the epitome of love, and just because his children happen to be contrary and unruly sometimes, that he will put them into eternal punishment. I can't see that. I'm a better father than that!

I believe that God is transcendent and at the same time immanent. I believe that God is a dynamic influence once we understand the idea of God— that God has set goals for us, and as we strive toward those goals, we make the world better, politically, socially, morally.

NOTES

1. Henry Franklin. C. L. Franklin refers to him hereafter as his father.
2. Rachel Franklin, C. L. Franklin's mother, recalls the incident: "We were getting ready to go to this school turnout, school program. The school was closing for that season, and he had a speech to say, and I had taken time and taught it to him, and told him just how I wanted him to stand on the stage, and how I wanted him to speak up so the people would hear him and understand what he was saying; and when they called him, he got up there and you couldn't hear him! You couldn't hear anything he said.

   "So I set there, you know, and looked at him. I just didn't know what was wrong. And I didn't say anything to him while we were at the school meeting. I waited until we got home. So when we got home, we all went in the house and undressed and everything, and he was kind of slow, because he knew what was fixing to happen, you know! He was kind of slow undressing, slow coming out of his room.

   "So I called him. And he came on out, and I said, 'What was wrong with you tonight? You never have spoke like that.' I said, 'Do you know nobody understood what you were saying?' And I said, 'You didn't even open your mouth. What is wrong?'

   "And he just dropped his head. I think he was very sorry he did that, you know? But I had to talk to him about it, and then I got ahold of him about it. Afterwards, I told him. I shook my finger. I said, 'From now on I bet you'll open your mouth!' And he has been opening it ever since. (Laughs.)" See also how Franklin incorporates this family story into *Hannah, the Ideal Mother*.
3. Reverend J. M. Gates, from Atlanta, who recorded more than one hundred short sermons on 78s in the late 1920s, was the most popular recorded black preacher of his era, just as Franklin was the most popular of his. "Dead Cat on the Line" was a mock-sermon in which Gates inveighed, "If a child doesn't favor his father, there's a dead cat on the line!" Franklin does not believe that Gates's preaching had any influence on his own; instead, he patterned his style after the preachers he saw and heard in church as a boy.
4. Rachel Franklin recalled, "I knew that Clarence was going to be chosen for something, but I just didn't have it on my mind that he was going to

be a minister. Because he was so different. He never would just be ready to play with the other kids, but he would love for them to come around and be company. But to get down and shoot marbles like the kids used to do when he was a kid, he never did that. But he would make them welcome to do that. And he would love for them to come around. He was kind of a peculiar child. He would sit to himself, and sit there and enjoy looking at the other kids."

5. Rachel Franklin: "Clarence joined the church when he was quite young, quite young. I talked to him about getting over on the Lord's side, joining the church. And you don't know when the Lord is going to call you home, and you want to be a Christian. But I believe these things were already in his heart. I believe they were because I didn't have any trouble much on that at all. He was willing to be a member of the church. The prayers he wanted to pray, he would always tell me. He called me Aunt Rachel—all three of my children called me Aunt Rachel, like my sister's children—and he said, 'Aunt Rachel, I want you to sing one of the hymns,' say, 'I love to hear you sing,' and say, 'I want to sing like you sing and I want to pray like you.' "

6. Franklin had not mentioned this dream or vision in recounting how he became a preacher, when he spoke in February, 1976 and in the fall of 1977; I learned about it from Rachel Franklin, who said: "I had been sick for a good while, with malaria. And he went to church that night—he would always go to church, and when I was able, we both went together—so he came back from service that night and he got up and told me, 'I was called to preach last night.'

"And I lie there and say, 'What?'

"He say, 'Yes, I was called to preach.'

"And his planks was the tongue and groove, and he say, 'One of the little planks in my room was on fire, and a voice out of that fire called me and told me to go and preach the gospel to each and every nation.' And he say, 'I'm going to preach. I'm going to preach.' And you know I was very happy, very happy after he told me that."

The next time I spoke with Franklin, I told him what his mother had said. Thereupon he gave this version of the incident. I do not believe he held it back because he felt I would be unsympathetic; quite the opposite. Rather, having changed from a fundamentalist to a liberal Christian, he gave more credit to his growing deep conviction that he was called to preach than to this spectacular dream or vision.

7. Rachel Franklin: "He was to preach one Wednesday night at St. Peter's Rock in Mississippi—his first time preaching. People were there, the church was packed to hear him preach his first sermon. I was sitting there, looking happy as I could be, and looking on as he explained his text and lined out everything that he wanted in his sermon, and it was just amazing. He preached that night like he had been preaching for seven or eight years."

8. An African American who was the heavyweight boxing champion of the world from 1908 to 1915.
9. That is, the chief of the opposition to Franklin was Pugh.
10. Rachel Franklin recalls, "His father wanted him to be home, at work. And he told his father, 'Now you've got to turn me a-loose, because I cannot plow a mule and preach the gospel.' Said, 'You've got to let me go.'

   "So his father told him, said, 'All right.' Said, 'You make up your mind what you want to do. If you want to preach, preach.' "
11. Dorothy Swan characterizes Franklin's Mississippi attitude toward preaching as "wanting to tickle Grandma on the street." There he thought he was doing well to whoop and get people shouting in response.
12. Erma (born in Mississippi; "the baby" on p. 13), Cecil, Aretha, and Carolyn (all born in Memphis).
13. At St. Peter's Rock each member was called by name, came forward, gave his contribution, and the amount was announced publicly.
14. This was a difficult time for New Bethel and for Franklin; the church could not afford to pay him a salary, and he began to accept more invitations to preach at other churches. Under these conditions the real-estate man's offer was a greater temptation than otherwise.
15. The choice of which number to play in the daily policy game often was made on the basis of one's own or someone else's reported dream or vision. Dream books translated dream events and objects seen into numbers. If Lofton said, "I saw shoes," a person looked up shoes in the dream book to find the number to play. Lofton, of course, pretended not to know this was going on. But because of it, Lofton and Jones had large congregations and offerings, particularly from people whose numbers had come up.
16. Franklin had proposed that they have the broadcast without him preaching on it.
17. Dr. Reuben Gayden, who held classes for preachers in Franklin's home for a number of years.
18. It peaked at about 10,000 in the late 1950s, at the height of Franklin's popularity. Because of his broadcast, recordings, and preaching tours, visitors to Detroit always worshiped at New Bethel. Another reason for the congregation's growth was Franklin's personal appearance. He was such a flashy dresser, Dorothy Swan said, that people called him "black beauty" and "the jitterbug preacher."
19. The old Oriole Theater, a cavernous building that seats about 3000, on the corner of Linwood and Philadelphia Streets.
20. In 1977–78 the church had about 2000 members.
21. Barbara's death from a heart attack left Franklin as mother and father both to his children. With no permanent church home it was even more difficult for the Franklins, as the church did not pay him a salary, though by this time he was beginning to earn money from contributions to the radio broadcasts. Later in 1952 Franklin's stepfather died, and his

mother, Rachel, moved in to help him care for the children some time later. But Dorothy Swan remembers him calling her up one day before his mother moved in, when he was "stretching beans"—living cheaply on beans. "I keep cooking them and they just get harder and harder," he said. "Put water in them!" Dorothy replied.

22. She was the leader of the Clara Ward Gospel Singers, the best-known and most successful professional black gospel group in the post-World War II era.

23. Joe Von Battle, a Detroit record-store owner and record producer.

24. A western suburb of Detroit.

25. WLAC-AM.

26. Clara Ward's mother.

27. The Davis Sisters and the Hummingbirds were among the most popular professional black gospel groups of the 1950s.

28. At New Bethel, and in other Detroit Baptist churches, the minister waits until shortly before the sermon to walk into the sanctuary and take his seat on the pulpit. In some churches, the pastor sits in his office, watching the service on closed-circuit television, until it is time for him to enter.

29. That is, he preached on the same text, and used the same title. The sermon itself was not a carbon copy of the record, though it contained many of the same ideas.

30. A trustee of New Bethel.

31. Thomas Shelby, director of music at New Bethel.

32. U.S. Representative John Conyers.

33. *Elder* is the title by which black Pentecostals call their ministers. To call Franklin by the Pentecostal title instead of his own Baptist title is a sign of the visitors' insensitivity.

Selected Sermons of
Clarence LaVaughn Franklin

Introduction

Some may wonder why oral sermons belong in a book. Implicit is the criticism that, reduced to print, they are pale copies of the originals. The usual answer given with oral literature is that print captures the word forever; what would have been lost had not the Homeric poets written down the oral traditions of *The Iliad* and *The Odyssey,* for example? And, while the African American oral sermon tradition is vigorous, few of its contemporary exponents are as celebrated as Franklin was. With the fate of his sermon recordings uncertain, it seems wise to commit the texts to print at this time, for they will have a certain permanence.

But more than that, literary politics is involved. For decades, African American writers have testified that the church is a major fount of black culture, and that the preachers' sermons comprise a literature unparalleled in influence and excellence. Yet the African American sermon does not appear in the standard anthologies of American literature. Until recently its absence could be attributed as much to racism as to a lack of available written versions. But today, when the canon at last is opening to include more from women and minority writers, it is vital to have authentic, accurately transcribed texts or "scores" that evoke something of the power of the oral originals. This book is an effort to provide those texts in the hope that the African American sermon will take its rightful place in the American literary canon.

Seventy-five of Franklin's sermons, some in multiple versions, most oral and a few written, will appear in volume one of the larger work from which this book is excerpted. I selected the following twenty based on record sales, the advice of Franklin's daughter Erma and his secretary, Fannie Tyler, and my own judgment. Eighteen come from commercial, long-playing record albums made from about 1953 through 1974; most now, sadly, out of print. Two more are from my field recordings. All recordings were made in the natural context of the church's worship service where, for so celebrated a preacher, microphones and recordings were routine.

Most of these sermons come from Franklin's peak recording period in the mid-1950s. Grouping them in chronological order shows that in his later sermons Franklin grew increasingly interested in history and psychology. He paid ever more attention to the biblical characters that filled his sermons, treating them like real people, yet intrepreting them in the context of their time and place. He worked up his subjects lovingly. His themes did not change; but his sermons, always lucid, grew deeper as he grew wiser.

His sermons were extemporaneous but not spontaneous; he told me that he prepared carefully. Based on his seminary training, he selected a Scripture passage, looked up what the Bible commentaries said on it (he mentioned *The Interpreter's Bible* and *The Abingdon Bible Commentary* as his two main sources), wrote notes on the commentaries, then pondered his topic. After several days, he organized the sermon around the passage, deciding what would be the introduction, the body, and the summary or climax. He preached on several Scripture passages repeatedly over the years; in so doing, he was like the poet or composer who continually revises his works. His seminary teachers accepted both extemporaneous preaching and manuscript preaching, emphasizing preparation in both cases. Franklin chose to preach without notes because he felt he could keep better contact with his congregation if he looked at them.

Prior to delivering a sermon he studied a topical outline he had written on a piece of scrap paper or an index card; he kept it in his pocket while he delivered the sermon. His outline for *Without a Song* reads as follows:

> Without a song
>   Singers
>   Introduction
>   Singing a distinguishing characteristic of man
>   The effects that enslavement has upon oppressed peoples
>   Israel should have sung
>   The Negro sung in the night

One of the most important questions I faced in preparing this work was how to represent Franklin's oral sermons on the page. In this book I represent his spoken words in prose and his chanted and sung words in free verse. Centuries ago, when Protestant sermons were popular literature, they were written in prose, whether by ministers preparing beforehand or by transcribers during delivery. Today, the prose convention serves ministers and denominational publishing houses. But poets, novelists, folklorists, and anthropologists represent much of oral literature, particularly song, as verse.

When he saw my verse transcriptions, Franklin smiled and said that while a sermon might be written out in prose beforehand, as a representation of thoughts, it was transformed in delivery to something else, and this might well be represented as poetry. I represent Franklin's "whooping" (chant and song) in free verse for those reasons and another—meter. In the African American sermon, the chanted and sung portions, while unrhymed and not strictly regular in meter, have the rhythmic force of the regularly repeated event: the preacher "whoops" in a predictable melody, and this is followed by cries from the congregation, precisely on the tonic pitch. And again. And again. I asked Franklin about the rhythm of his climax. "It's not something I can tap my foot to," he said, "but I can feel it; it's in me." Free verse better represents "whooping's" event-centered meter than prose.

Yet prose, I think, best conveys Franklin's spoken oratory. He told me he spoke during the first several minutes of a sermon in order to reach the hearers' intellect, then "whooped" during the climax to reach their emotions. When we discussed the transcriptions, he said he preferred prose for the spoken sections, and would accept poetry for the "whooped" ones. This supports the traditional distinction between expository argument, for which Western writers conventionally employ prose, and the language whose power eclipses logic—poetry. Franklin had logical exposition in mind when he spoke in the pulpit. And although these spoken sections involve storytelling, he did not intend them as imitations of life, nor as flights of poetic fancy. Setting spoken sections as verse would indeed highlight the poetic aspects of Franklin's oratory: parallelism, metaphor, dramatic timing. But it would also obscure the distinction between two modes of performance that are differently intended, delivered, received, and understood.

The sources for my transcriptions are Franklin's commercial recordings for the JVB, Battle, Chess, and Jewel recording companies; and my field recordings. Most of his words are easily audible, but as he left the microphone from time to time while "whooping," occasional words and phrases were impossible for me to hear, and these I have marked with a question mark in brackets: [?]. I must have misheard some words and, although I have had others spot-check my transcriptions, I take full responsibility for any errors and hope that they are few.

An exegetical rather than a topical preacher, Franklin based each sermon on a biblical passage, quoting it from the King James Version at the outset of the sermon. Occasionally he quoted from other versions. On those few occasions when he misquoted slightly, I have let what he said stand. I put direct addresses to the congregation such as "Are you praying with me?" in parenthesis. Franklin told me he used them to gain time, to ask for more amens from the congregation, and to get them to pay better attention. The congregation members knew what he wanted and responded more fully—for a while, at any rate.

For reasons of economy I cannot show a melody for each "whooped" section, nor can I show the cries of response from the congregation—they must be imagined; but I put the "whooped" portion of one sermon, *The Eagle Strirreth Her Nest,* in musical notation in the forthcoming work. Franklin's melody follows a similar pattern in each of his sermons, and I used that pattern as a guide in setting up the poetic lines in each sermon.

I divide Franklin's "whooping" into lines based on his pauses for breath; that is, I stop each line where he stops for breath and I begin again on the line below where he begins again after taking a breath. I start each line a particular distance from the left-hand side of the page depending on the shape of its melody. Three melodic shapes are prominent. The first is brief and formulaic (e.g., "O Lord"), tends to gain Franklin time, and establishes or reestablishes the tonal center by rising or falling quickly to the tonic. This type I call an "auxiliary" line and I set it flush against the left margin. Another type of line starts or quickly rises to the highest pitch and then falls toward the tonic, usually by thirds (e.g., 5-3-3-1). This type I call "main" and set it indented half an inch from the left margin. A third type of line follows a main line and has its highest pitch below the preceding main line's highest pitch, usually a minor third above the tonic, and then it usually ends on the tonic. This type I call a "secondary" line and set indented one inch from the left margin.

When he is "whooping," Franklin's syntax fills particular melodies; auxiliary lines are formulas or conjunctions; main lines carry subject and verb; secondary lines carry objects and prepositional phrases. This correspondence collapses near the sermon's close, when most lines have the highest pitch, become main lines, and carry all parts of speech.

Here is an example of some "whooped" lines from *A Mother at the Cross,* showing auxiliary lines flush left, main lines indented, and secondary liens indented further:

O Lord.	[auxiliary line]
And	[auxiliary line]
I remember reading	[main line]
a story a long time ago	[secondary line]
that dealt with	[secondary line]
mother's eternal love.	[main line]

Before each sermon I place a brief headnote. The headnote gives, first, the sermon's title; I take this from the commercial recording (if any) and any alternate titles. After that I give record company, the release number, and the date (if known) of the recording. A few of the commercially recorded sermons can be dated from within by Franklin's references to the year or to current events, but dating most of the sermons is a problem. Franklin could not date them precisely. I was unable to gain access to the late Joe Von Battle's files to see if he noted the dates of the sermons he recorded. Chess Records' discographer, Michel Ruppli, shows dates for some of the sermons from the Chess files, but these dates indicate when Chess acquired the sermons, often considerably later than when they were initially recorded.

1

The Eagle Stirreth Her Nest

Chess LP-21.
Recorded ca. 1953.
His most popular sermon recording;
Erma Franklin thinks it his best.

[Franklin probably began by reading Deuteronomy 32:11–12.] The eagle stirreth her nest.

The eagle here is used to symbolize God's care and God's concern for his people. Many things have been used as symbolic expressions to give us a picture of God or some characteristic of one of his attributes: the ocean, with her turbulent majesty; the mountains, the lions. Many things have been employed as pictures of either God's strength or God's power or God's love or God's mercy. And the psalmist has said that The heavens declare the glory of God and the firmament shows forth his handiworks.

So the eagle here is used as a symbol of God. Now in picturing God as an eagle stirring her nest, I believe history has been one big nest that God has been eternally stirring to make man better and to help us achieve world brotherhood. Some of the things that have gone on in your own experiences have merely been God stirring the nest of your circumstances. Now the Civil War, for example, and the struggle in connection with it, was merely the promptings of Providence to lash man to a point of being brotherly to all men. In fact, all of the wars that we have gone through, we have come out with new outlooks and new views and better people. So that throughout history, God has been stirring the various nests of circumstances surrounding us, so that he could discipline us, help us to know ourselves, and help us to love another, and to help us hasten on the realization of the kingdom of God.

The eagle symbolizes God because there is something about an eagle that is a fit symbol of things about God. In the first place, the eagle is the king of fowls. And if he is a regal or kingly bird, in that majesty he represents the kingship of God or symbolizes the kingship of God. (Listen if you please.) For God is not merely a king, he is *the* king. Somebody has said that he is the king of kings. For you see, these little kings that we know, they've got to have a king over them. They've got to account to somebody for the deeds done in their bodies. For God is *the* king. And if the eagle is a kingly bird, in that way he symbolizes the regalness and kingliness of our God.

In the second place, the eagle is strong. Somebody has said that as the eagle goes winging his way through the air he can look down on a young lamb grazing by a mountainside, and can fly down and just with the strength of his claws, pick up this young lamb and fly away to yonder's cleft and devour it—because he's strong. If the eagle is strong, then, in that he is a symbol of God, for our God is strong. Our God is strong. Somebody has called him a fortress. So that when the enemy is pursuing me I can run behind him. Somebody has called him a citadel of protection and redemption. Somebody else has said that he's so strong until they call him a leaning-post that thousands can lean on him, and he'll never get away. (I don't believe you're praying with me.) People have been leaning on him ever since time immemorial. Abraham leaned on him. Isaac and Jacob leaned on him. Moses and the prophets leaned on him. All the Christians leaned on him. People are leaning on him all over the world today. He's never given way. He's strong. That's strong. Isn't it so?

In the second place, he's swift. The eagle is swift. And it is said that he could fly with such terrific speed that his wings can be heard rowing in the air. He's swift. And if he's swift in that way, he's a symbol of our God. For our God is swift. I said he's swift. Sometimes, sometimes he'll answer you while you're calling him. He's swift. Daniel was thrown in a lions' den. And Daniel rung him on the way to the lions' den. And having rung him, why, God had dispatched the angel from heaven. And by the time that Daniel got to the lions' den, the angel had changed the nature of lions and made them lay down and act like lambs. He's swift. Swift. One night Peter was put in jail and the church went down on its knees to pray for him. And while the church was praying, Peter knocked on the door. God was so swift in answering prayer. So that if the eagle is a swift bird, in that way he represents or symbolizes the fact that God is swift. He's swift. If you get in earnest tonight and tell him about your troubles, he's swift to hear you. All you do is need a little faith, and ask him in grace.

Another thing about the eagle is that he has extraordinary sight. Extraordinary sight. Somewhere it is said that he can rise to a lofty height in the air and look in the distance and see a storm hours away. That's extraordinary sight. And sometimes he can stand and gaze right in the sun because he has extraordinary sight. I want to tell you my God has extraordinary sight. He can see every ditch that you have dug for me and guide me around them. God has extraordinary sight. He can look behind that smile on your face and see that frown in your heart. God has extraordinary sight.

Then it is said that an eagle builds a nest unusual. It is said that the eagle selects rough material, basically, for the construction of his nest. And then as the nest graduates toward a close or a finish, the material becomes finer and softer right down at the end. And then he goes about to set up residence in that nest. And when the little eaglets are born, she goes out and brings in food to feed them. But when they get to the point where they're old enough to be out on their own, why, the eagle will begin to pull out some of that down and let some of those thorns come through so that the nest won't be, you know, so comfortable. So when they get to lounging around and rolling around, the thorns prick 'em here and there. (Pray with me if you please.)

I believe that God has to do that for us sometimes. Things are going so well and we are so satisfied that we just lounge around and forget to pray. You'll walk around all day and enjoy God's life, God's health and God's strength, and go climb into bed without saying, "Thank you, Lord, for another day's journey." We'll do that. God has to pull out a little of the plush around us, a little of the comfort around us, and let a few thorns of trial and tribulation stick through the nest to make us pray sometime. Isn't it so? For most of us forget God when things are going well with us. Most of us forget him.

It is said that there was a man who had a poultry farm. And that he raised chickens for the market. And one day in one of his broods he discovered a strange looking bird that was very much unlike the other chickens on the yard. [Whooping:]

And
>the man
>>didn't pay too much attention.
>But he noticed
>>as time went on
that
>this strange looking bird
>>was unusual.
>He outgrew
>>the other little chickens,
>his habits were stranger
>>and different.
O Lord.
>But he let him grow on,
>and let him mingle
>>with the other chickens.
O Lord.
>And then one day a man

who knew eagles
        when he saw them,
came along
        and saw that little eagle
        walking in the yard.
And
    he said to his friend,
    "Do you know
        that you have an eagle here?"
    The man said, "Well,
        I didn't really know it.
    But I knew he was different
        from the other chickens.
And
    I knew that his ways
        were different.
And
    I knew that his habits
        were different.
And
    he didn't act like
        the other chickens.
    But I didn't know
        that he was an eagle."
    But the man said, "Yes,
        you have an eagle here on your yard.
    And what you ought to do
        is build a cage.
    After while
    when he's a little older
        he's going to get tired
        of the ground.
Yes he will.
    He's going to rise up
        on the pinion of his wings.
Yes,
and
    as he grows,
why,
    you can change the cage,
and
    make it a little larger

        as he grows older
        and grows larger."
    The man went out
        and built a cage.
And
    every day he'd go in
        and feed the eagle.
But
    he grew
        a little older
        and a little older.
Yes he did.
    His wings
        began
    to scrape on the sides
        of the cage.
And
    he had to build
        another cage
    and open the door of the old cage
        and let him into
    a larger cage.
Yes he did.
O Lord.
And
    after a while
        he outgrew that one day
        and then he had to build
        another cage.
    So one day
        when the eagle had gotten grown,
Lord God,
    and his wings
        were twelve feet
        from tip to tip,
o Lord,
    he began to get restless
    in the cage.
Yes he did.
    He began to walk around
        and be uneasy.
Why,

he heard
       noises
       in the air.
A flock of eagles flew over
       and he heard
       their voices.
And
       though he'd never been around eagles,
       there was something about that voice
          that he heard
       that moved
          down in him,
       and made him
          dissatisfied.
O Lord.
And
       the man watched him
          as he walked around
          uneasy.
O Lord.
       He said, "Lord,
          my heart goes out to him.
       I believe I'll go
          and open the door
          and set the eagle free."
O Lord.
       He went there
          and opened the door.
Yes.
       The eagle walked out,
          yes,
       spreaded his wings,
          then took 'em down.
Yes.
       The eagle walked around
          a little longer,
and
       he flew up a little higher
          and went to the barnyard.
And,
yes,
       he set there for awhile.

He wiggled up a little higher
and flew in yonder's tree.
Yes.

And then he wiggled up a little higher
and flew to yonder's mountain.
Yes.
Yes!
Yes.

One of these days,
        one of these days.
My soul
        is an eagle
in the cage that the Lord
        has made for me.
My soul,
        my soul,
my soul
        is caged in,
        in this old body,
        yes it is,
and one of these days
the man who made the cage
will open the door
and let my soul
        go.
Yes he will.
You ought to
        be able to see me
        take the wings of my soul.
Yes, yes,
yes,
yes!
Yes, one of these days.
One of these old days.
One of these old days.
Did you hear me say it?
I'll fly away
        and be at rest.
Yes.
Yes!
Yes!
Yes!

Yes!
Yes.
One of these old days.
One of these old days.
And

    when troubles
        and trials are over,
    when toil
        and tears are ended,
    when burdens
        are through burdening,
    ohh!
    Ohh.
    Ohh!
    Ohh one of these days.
    Ohh one of these days.
    One of these days.
    One of these days,
    my soul will take wings,
    my soul will take wings.
    Ohh!
    Ohh, a few more days.
    Ohh, a few more days.
    A few more days.
    O Lord.

2

The Prodigal Son

Chess LP-23.
Recorded ca. 1954.

[Franklin probably began by reading Luke 15:11–32.] I don't believe that there is a greater love story in all of the Bible or in any literature printed, be it secular or sacred, there isn't a greater love story than the story of the prodigal son. Jesus dramatically tells of God's love and God's patience and God's long-suffering and God's concern about man in this passage.

He intended to show, first of all, the danger of self-righteousness in the characterization of the son that stayed at home. Although he stayed at home, although he did not go astray, although he did not engage in wild and riotous living, when his brother was redeemed and was regained, he was too selfish to come in and join in the banquet and celebrate the recovery of his lost brother. So that Jesus intends for us to learn in this that it is as dangerous to stay in the Church and be selfish as it is to go out but finally come back.

Now the theme of this passage is loss. And Jesus intended to show us that God is a God of the lost. Now Jesus also said that God was not the God of the living—or, rather, of the dead— but a God of the living. By that he did not mean that he turned his back on you when you die, but he really meant that no man is dead with God. And David had us to know that we cannot escape to any land where God is not. If he went into the heavens, if he went to the utmost parts of the earth, if he made his bed in hell, behold, God is there. So God is a God of the lost. If you do not believe that he's the God of the lost make up in your mind to come back to God, and like the father of the prodigal his arms will be wide open, and a robe will be waiting, you understand, in his wardrobe of blessings.

Now I said the theme of this story is loss. Jesus in this chapter tells of three things that were lost. First he tells of lost sheep. Secondly he tells of lost money. Thirdly he tells of a lost son. In the case of the lost sheep, the shepherd went back over his steps and over his traveling, the day, the previous day, and searched in every ravine and every mountainside and every valley until he had regained the sheep that was lost. The woman who lost one of her coins of ten swept in every corner and under every bed and behind every door until she had found her lost coin. But then there's no word of anybody having gone out to look for this lost son.

You see, in the case of the sheep we have the loss of property. In the case of the lost coin we have financial loss. In the case of the son we have human loss. People go out looking to regain lost property. People work double shifts in order to regain lost money. But very few people bother themselves about trying to regain lost sons, lost daughters, lost husbands or lost wives, or even lost friends.

This young man, in the case of the prodigal son, why, became restless, according to the story, and became a little impatient with the discipline and order and regulation of his home. Possibly his brother led a life that was too dull. Possibly the loving rule of his father was a little irritating. Yes, he was young, and the blood of youth was dancing for anxiety and excitement in his veins. You understand, his heart had grown alien, alien to his home, alien to the traditional situation among his people, alien to the things that were native to him. The far country of excitement beckoned to him. And he went to his father and petitioned him: "Father, give me all of the goods that fall to me."

His father did not hesitate. He immediately divided his living, you understand, and gave the young man his share. And not many days hence he took his journey into that far country. (Listen if you please.) He didn't go off looking for the young man, for the young man wasn't lost. Yes, he was lost. I don't mean only so far as morals, or so far as that which is spiritual is concerned. I mean he was lost from himself. So the record is that when he found himself in the pigpen, he came to himself, which means that he was not at himself when he left home. (I wished I had somebody here to pray with me.)

You see, there are situations in life—. Let me put it this way: I think sometimes that adversity helps us to find ourselves. Some of the folk, some of the folk who are sitting here, listening at me, have gone through experiences and know that there are times in your life when you thought you knew it all, when you thought that you could impose your way and your will upon everybody, when you thought that it was right to be selfish. For you see, the first law of Nature may be self first, but the first law of Grace is others first. (I wish I had somebody here praying with me tonight. Listen if you please.) And it took a little adversity, it took a little sickness, or it took a little misfortune, or it took a little shake-up in your life, to help you to find yourself.

You see, this young man didn't find himself until he had gone all the way from a palace to a pigpen. (Pray with me if you please.) Took his journey into a far country where he was alien: alien from God, alien from his friends, alien from his surroundings and from his native home. The wild blue yonder called and there was nothing at home that could satisfy him. Hence he took his journey into a far country, and the record is that he there wasted his living, or his substance in riotous living. Wasted.

Loss always follows waste. If you waste your money, one day you'll want it. (Did you hear what I said?) If you waste your influence, if you abuse your influence, one day you'll wish you had it. If you waste your health, one day you'll want it. For in every instance, loss always follows waste.

The record is that when this young man wasted his substance in riotous living, when he wasted that which had been given to him, then a mighty famine arose and he began to be in want. A mighty famine arose. For you see, famines are still rising. It might not have been an economic famine or it might not be an economic famine in all instances. Sometimes it is the famine of health. A famine may be going on with you in your home and in your community and not necessarily going on with anybody else.

This young man had gone to this far country and no doubt had received a warm reception. When he came in as a prince of an Eastern rich man, with his diamond necklaces, with his gold bracelets, with his servants, with his camels and with all of his flock, why, no doubt the far country of his desire received him with open arms. For when you don't need anything you always can get anything you want. If you have a car anybody will let you ride. If you have money anybody will lend you some money. But if it gets around that you are broke the story is different. (I wish somebody would pray with me.)

This young man dissipated not only his body, and listen if you please, he dissipated everything else that he had. And, you know, there are a lot of people who think and who talk about how expensive it is to be a member of the church. I want to serve notice on you tonight, it's far more expensive to follow after the ways of the world than it is to be a child of God. For when you get with the crowd out yonder, you're all right as long as you can help bear the load. You're all right as long as you can contribute to the pot. You're all right as long as you can order everybody to sit up. But when it gets to the place where you can't do that, the world is through with you.

If you don't believe I'm telling you the truth, go with me to one of the tuberculosis sanitariums tonight. And talk with, walk with me around with many a young man, and many a young woman, and they will tell you as long as things were going well, they could not sleep for the telephone. They had to be at every party. But when they had wasted all, when the famine of health rose in their lives, the telephone doesn't ring any more. And on visiting day, that crowd of slaves that they used to run with are conspicuously missing. (I wish I had somebody here to pray with me.)

Yes, but listen, brothers and sisters. This young man was reduced to a very shameful level for a man of his nationality. Only a Jew could tell you how he felt about tying himself to a Gentile master in these far-off days and having to work among swine. The young man sat there, you understand, in the hogpen. [Whooping:]

> He sat there
>> hungry
> and set there
>> you understand
> full of experience and wisdom that he'd gained
>> from all of his trials.
> And as he sat there
>> thinking about it,
> hungry
> and realizing
> that he'd come from
>> a palace
>> down to a pigpen,
> and in this situation,
> the record is
>> he came to himself.
> I wish somebody tonight
>> that's listening to me
> would sit right where you are
>> and come to yourself.

O Lord.

> You know Jesus told
>> this story
> in order to let men know
> that he had faith
>> in men,
> that he did not believe that man
>> was ultimately
>> sinful
>> and wicked,
> but the ultimate end
>> of man was
>> to come to God.
> For you see, my brothers
>> and my sisters,
> to do wrong

                    is alien with man.
One of these days
                    wrongness
                    will disappear.
One of these days
                    selfishness
                    will be wiped out on this globe.
One of these days
                    wars
                    will end,
and

one of these days peace
                    will prevail.
(I don't believe you know what I'm talking about.)
And this young man
                    sat there,
realizing
                    that he had ended up there
                    and was paying for his folly.
O Lord.
He sat there,
                    there among swines,
with hogs
                    all around him.
O Lord.
Realizing,
great God,
                    that he'd sought a freedom
                    without laws,
o Lord,
                    that he wanted a freedom
                    at the expense
                    of law and order
                    and discipline,
o Lord,
                    and he'd given up a
                    happy home.
You ought to be able
                    to see him sitting there
                    thinking to himself:
Here I am
                    in rags,

                        in tattered rags,
            but at home my father
                        has a wardrobe
                        full of robes.
            Here I am
                        with the last bracelet gone,
and
            in my father's jewelry box
                        there's another bracelet there.
O Lord.
            Here I am
                        with no necklace
                        about my neck,
            and at my father's house
                        there are many necklaces,
o Lord.
            And here I am hungry,
                        yeah,
            and at home
                        there's bread
                        and enough to spare.
O Lord.
            I know
                        that I've done wrong,
yes,
            I know,
                        yes,
                        yes I know,
            I know
                        I disobeyed my father,
            I know
                        that I'm a violator,
            I know
                        that I've been wild
                        and then I've been reckless,
yes I have,
            but I'm going
                        back home today.
O Lord.
            I've done wrong
                        but I'm going home,
                        yes I am.

I'm a rioter
> but I'm going home,
> yes I am.

I'm hungry
> but I'm going home,

yes I am.

I'm outdoors
> but I'm going home,

yes.

> Yes!
> (I wish somebody would pray with me.)
> Yes.
> Yes.
> I'm going to tell my father,

yes,

> that Lord, Father,
> > Father,
> Father!

yes,

> Father!

yes,

> I've been wrong,
> > yes I have,
> Father!
> > I know I disobeyed you,

yes I did,

> I left home talking about
> > give me,
> I left home telling you
> > to give me,
> but I've come back home today,
> telling you to make me,
> make me
> > one of your servants,

o Lord.

> And that's what I'm telling them now.
> Lord!
> Lord.
> Lord!
> Lord!
> You just make me,
> you just make me,

as one of your highest servants.
Lord!
Lord.
Lord!
Lord!
Lord.
Lord!
Just use me,
anything you want me to do,
here is my life,
here is my heart,
here are my hands,
here are my eyes,
Lord!
Lord.
Lord!
O Lord.
Ohh!
Ohh yes!
Yes!
Just make me
one of your highest servants,
yes.

3

Pressing On

Chess LP-42.
Recorded in 1955.

In the book of Philippians, the third chapter, thirteenth and fourteenth verses, we will find this passage: "Brethren, I count not myself to have apprehended: but this one thing I do, forgetting the things which are behind, and reaching forth unto those things which are before, I press toward the mark for the prize of the high calling which is in Christ Jesus."

Pressing on. Pressing on.

Paul addressed this letter to a group of Philippian Christians, people who had recently subscribed to the way of Christ and of God. We call your attention to the humility of this great apostle. We say that he was great. In fact, we think—and many Bible students and scholars rate him next to Jesus as a preacher, for it was he who interpreted the Christian idea to the world. For Paul not only preached, but his ability rendered him able to write and therefore interpret this to the reading world—the Christian idea.

And so in his epistle to these Christians, I want you first to consider not only his humility, but his sense of brotherliness. "Brethren, I count not myself to have apprehended." Not only am I humble in my advice, and in what I have to offer you, but I consider you as my brothers, brethren. Listen at this great scholar who can speak several languages fluently, who could speak, or preach in Athens as easily as in Jerusalem, his own native capital, a man who could address the philosophical Greeks, a man who could interpret and who had done a job for the Christian idea that we cannot even understand. And yet not only was he a scholar, not only was he capable of speaking several languages, but he was a Jew, and more than a mere vagabond Jew, he was a Pharisee. And with all of these things to his credit, he declared, "I count not myself to have apprehended." Most of us can't stand having a little, not to mention all of this, to our credit before we get our heads too big for our bodies.

But this year, 1955, we ought to think in terms of brotherhood. We ought to think in terms of humility. (Pray with me if you please.)

"I count not myself to have apprehended." Paul gives himself credit for only one thing. He points up the fact that I have only one thing that I can boast of: that I am able to forget the things behind and press on toward the things which are before. That, our great radio preacher for the National Council of Churches called this "Looking backwards in order to live forwards." But you see too many people look backwards and live backwards. (Pray with me.) Not only do they look back to the past, but they live in the past. Some folk can't do anything today, for reveling and boasting about what they used to do. Some people are bragging so much about what they did for the church, I heard one good member say, "Well, I'm going to set down now, for I've done enough." When have you gotten to the place that you've done enough in the service of God?

Paul was not able to say that until he came to the end. When he came to the end, only then did he say, "I've fought a good fight. I've kept the faith, I've finished my course." You haven't done too much. If you are looking back with a view of guiding yourself for the future, it's good to look back. But if the past inhibits your service, if you cannot look back without going back at least in your mind, you ought to press on and look forward. (I wished I had somebody here praying with me. Listen if you please. Listen if you please.)

If there's something in the past that shackles you, if there's something in the past that mixes you up, then don't look back at least at that. You who are trying to build a family, you who are trying to build homes, you who are at least going to try to stay together, don't keep on looking back on things that corrupt your relationship. Don't keep on looking back. You who consider yourselves Christians, you who have been in some church and some little upheaval arose, and you have stopped working, stopped doing your job because you can't help but look back on the old church fight, you ought to quit looking back and come on back and join the army and press on toward the mark. (I wish you'd pray with me, I wish you'd pray with me.)

Paul said—. You see, it takes a little growth, it takes a little strength, it takes takes a little love, it takes a little God to say, "I'm able to forget the things that are behind and press on to the things that are before." Yes, there are some good things in the past. History is a record of the past. Many good things. Possibly you have done a number of good things in the past. We are not trying to discredit what you have done or what your achievements have been in the past. We're simply saying, don't stagnate your growth and don't stagnate your possibilities by satisfying yourself with what you have done in the past. For whatever you've done in the past, you can do so many other good things in the future. And there are so many more things to do in the future. Isn't it so?

So like Paul, you ought to feel brotherly. You ought to feel humble. You ought to have only one thing to boast about, and that's you're able to untie yourself from the past, you're able to cut off yourself from your weaknesses in the past, from your shortcomings in the past, from your mistakes of the past, and press on to be a better man, a better woman, a better child of God in the future than you've been in the past. (I don't believe you're praying with me.)

No wonder the songwriter says,

I'm pressing on that upward way,
New heights I'm gaining, every day;
Still praying as I onward bound,
Lord, plant my feet on higher ground.
Lord, lift me up, Lord, let me stand
By faith, on heaven's table land,
A higher place than I have found;
Lord, plant my feet on higher ground.

(Pray with me if you please.) Yes, there have been valleys in the past, there have been mountains in the past, there have been problems in the past, there have been trials and tests in the past—(pray with me if you please)—but if you'll look before you, you'll think with the hymnologist as he says,

So many snares were set for me,
    and mountains in my way,
that in 1955 if Jesus will my leader be,
    I'll make it home someday.

Yes, there are curves in the future that I've got to go around. There's rough roads that I've got to go around in the future. There are mountains to be climbed in the future. There are enemies to encounter in the future. Satan and his hosts will meet me in the future.

I'm going to close with this story. I remember having heard a story of a young sprinter who became a world renowned runner. This young man had won every local victory, had won every statewide victory, had won every national victory, had won even the international victory. And one day while walking around in a foreign city, [whooping:]

he ran across an old man.
    The old man approached him,
said to him, "I understand that you
    are that young runner.
I understand that you are the young man
    who won all the laurels."
The young man said, "Well,

I guess you have heard of me."
But he said, "I'd like to challenge you
            to a race.
I'd like to
            get a run with you."
The young man looked on the old man
            in disgust
and said, "Do you mean to tell me,
and here you are with your head white,
and with your body having been touched by old age,
time having plowed furrows in your face,
that you would put yourself up to run with me,
knowing my victories,
knowing my triumphs as a runner?"
I heard the old man say, "Well,
it's not going to hurt you.
Certainly can't do you any harm.
And if you aren't afraid, run with me."
After a long argument and after much discussed,
the young man said, "Well, the track is just
            up the streets.
I know where a track is.
I'll run
            with you a little while."
[He] went in and said, "Let me dress and get myself together."
The young man went in to dress and the old man went in
                                    and dressed also.
They walked out on the track and as some timekeeper rang
                                    the gong,
the young man started out in his usual graceful style,
striding along with all of the grace and poise
            that an athlete could employ.
But as he strided along,
the old man
            strided along with him.
As he ran along, my brothers and sisters,
the old man ran
            at his side.
And
            as he went around the first bend
                        the young man decided
            that he was going

to put on a little more speed,

for

it was usually his custom,

holy God,

why,

to wait until
the first lap of the race
before he got ready to go in.

O Lord.

But as he put on
a little more speed,
the old man
picked up a little more himself.

And

as the young man looked to his side,
he saw the old man still
striding by his side.
And then
as they ran on
a little more,

why,

the young man
put on a little more speed,
but the old man
also put on speed.
He ran
a little further,

and

he got a little faster,
but the old man
got a little faster also.
And in the home stretch
he put on
all that he had.

O Lord.

But the old man
was still by his side.

O Lord.

And when they got near
the finish line,

o Lord,

the old man ran out

in the lead
and ran across
the finish line
ahead of the young man.
The young man
was astonished.
The young man
was outdone.
He sat down and said,
"Do you mind telling me
who you are?
And what is your name?
An old man at your age,
outrunning me?"
O Lord.
The old man set down
with confidence on his brow,
and said,
"You mean to tell me,
that you don't know who I am?
Set down
and I'll tell you.
Yes, I know you're a famous runner,
but I myself am also
a famous runner.
I've had
many a race,
and I, too,
have never lost a race."
The young man said, "Well,
why haven't I
heard about you?"
O Lord.
The old man said, "Well,
you've heard about me,
but you just don't know who I am.
O Lord.
I outran Abraham,
Isaac and Jacob,
yes I did.
I caught up with Moses,
and I outran all

of the prophets,
yes I did.
Great men
have been run down by me.
Wise men
have never been able
to outrun me.
O Lord.
And then one day on Calvary,
I caught up with Jesus,
yes I did.
For my name
is Death,
yes it is.
My name
is Death."
Lord, Lord.
Yes.
And I want to tell you,
as I go to my seat tonight,
I want to tell you,
I want to tell you
that I'm in the race
tonight,
yes I am.
I'm running
every day.
Yes.
I know there's a runner
by my side.
Yes.
Every,
every,
every,
every day,
every day,
yes,
I'm running,
down the track of life,
every day,
oh every day.
Every day,

yes,
ohh,
every day,
I'm running, yes I am,
but I know
that one of these old days
the race will be over,
yes it will.
One of these days,
one of these days,
yes!
Yes.
Yes!
Yes!
One of these days
the race will be over.

4

How Long Halt Ye
between Two Opinions?

[*Israel in the Throes of Indecision;
Elijah and Baal*].
Battle 6111. Recorded mid-1950s.
Reissued on Chess LP-63.

I call your attention to the first book of the Kings in the eighteenth chapter, the twenty-first verse: "And Elijah came unto all the people, and said, How long halt ye between two opinions? If God be God, follow him; if Baal, then follow him. And the people answered him not a word."

Israel in the throes of indecision. Israel in the throes of indecision.

(You haven't started to going to sleep already, have you? Wait a few minutes!)

It seems that this was in the eighth century of Israel's existence as a nation. Not too long since, Israel had been a nomadic, wandering people. Later they had become a pastoral people, but now under the leadership of General Joshua, they had successfully invaded Canaan, and had become exposed to a higher type of civilization. They had become exposed to urban and city dwelling life. And they had automatically taken on some of the ways of these city-dwellers, and these rulers whose gods were Baal. This had displeased the prophets who were zealous and who were jealous about maintaining the way of life that Israel had known, this close, tribal brotherhood, this zealousness toward Yahweh, or God. And of course with Israel ever expanding and taking on new responsibilities involved in nationhood—for when a people have been nomads, and swiftly go through the transition of taking on the responsibilities of running a nation, this automatically changes their lives.

And this change displeased the prophets, particularly the prophet Elijah. To him this amounted to apostasy, to him this amounted to backsliding, to them this meant that they were turning their back on Yahweh or God, and embracing the way of the Baals, the gods of the country. (Are you praying?) And so Elijah observed that not only had the practice of Baalism crept into the worship of Yahweh, with its ceremony, with its ritual or liturgy, but he saw that for political expediency the king, Ahab, had married one of the daughters of a king whose god was Baal. Her name was Jezebel. (I don't believe you're going to pray with me tonight.) And of course he had entered into certain agreements with her father and with her to permit her to import her god and her form of worship into Yahweh's country, into God's land. And to a degree this not only made the worship of Baal attractive, it made it official because the queen worshiped this god. And you know there are people who do not think about what they are doing, they think about only what is popular, and what other people are doing.

And of course the prophet Elijah went up to register his protest. The prophet went up to rebuke the king. The prophet went up to challenge this practice, the very fact that this was permitted in Yahweh's land. And of course he didn't stand around to vindicate his stand or his position; in this connection he went on away, depending upon God to look after him. And of course he had prophesied that unless this practice ceased, God had made it known to him, God had revealed to him that he would withhold the rain and the dew from the heavens above for three years and six months. And of course, naturally, this must have sounded fanatical to the king and to the court. It was meaningless to Jezebel. And the prophet must have looked foolish to the courtiers. But you know God sometimes does things in such a way that does not meet our popular standards, does not comply with our approaches and our way of doing things.   [Whooping:]

> But then ere long, as the prophet had predicted,
> the fields began to turn dry,
> the grass began to wither,
> the flowers faded,
> the rivers receded
>   and dried up,
> the lakes dried up,
> the cattle lowed as it were from the hillside,
> for the want of water,
> but there was no water to be found.
> Certain men were appointed
>   to take the cattle
> and lead them to distant places
>   to find water.
> Meanwhile the court remembered
> this old fanatical prophet
> who had come in
>   and who had made this protest

and who had uttered this prophecy.
When they couldn't find him,
  their anxiety
  increased.
Eventually
the prophet heard
  that they were in search for him,
and God urged upon him
  that the time was ripe
  for him to go back
  and reappear
  before the king.
  And upon his appearance
he met one of the king's chiefs,
  Obadiah.
And when Obadiah recognized him,
why, he became afraid,
when the prophet said, "Go tell the king
  that I'm here,
  that I'm back."
But Obadiah said, "I can't go,
because if I leave you the Spirit may come upon you,
  and you may disappear."
But I heard him say, "As the Lord liveth,
  I'll be here.
I came purposely
  to see the king."
When the king met him,
  in an effort to shift the responsibility
  from himself,
he said, "Art thou he
who troubles
  all Israel?"
But the prophet had him to know
that, "It's not me, king.
  It's you.
It's these foreign alliances,
these new entanglements,
these new allegiances,
  that you have formed
with these foreigners
  and their strange religion.

These things are
                offensive
                to our God.
And now
                I want to,
                I want to
                pose a proposition to you.
Now if God is real
                we may as well know it.
We may as well prove it.
If God is real
                we may as well establish it.
If Baal on the other hand
                is real,
we may as well establish that.
Now I know the great influence
                that Baal wields in this nation.
I know the great popularity
                that Baal has
                in this community.

And

I'd like to pose this proposition
that we'll call the nation together
                up on the summit of Mount Carmel
and that we'll try these gods
                by fire.
I am willing
                to take a stand with Yahweh,
                or with God.

And

those who are with Baal
                may take their stand with him.
We'll build an altar
and the god that answers
                by fire,
let him
                be God.
Let him be
                the official God.
Let him be
                the God of the nation.
Let him be the God

that the nation is ready
 to serve and respect
 and to cast their allegiance with.
How long will you halt
 between two opinions?
How long will you vacillate
 between Baal and Yahweh?
How long will you remain
undecided
as to who is God,
 Baal or Yahweh?"

[Speaking:] (I don't believe you're going to pray with me.) This proposition was ultimately accepted. And of course the nation met on Mount Carmel. Of course the prophets of Baal met out there, about eight hundred strong, dressed in impressive regalia, with beautiful ritual or liturgy. They went through their ceremony that I'm sure was attractive and impressive to the nation. They built their altars and they went through all of the things that they usually went through during their ritual, calling on the god of Baal. [Whooping:]

And they called him
 from morning until noon,
begging him
 to answer,
begging him to rain down fire,
and burn up
 the altar.
But you see Baal
 was the type of god
 that seems to prevail
 in our minds today,
 that seems to prevail in our thinking today.
Baal was an unrealistic god.
Baal was a god that had eyes
 that could not see,
 ears that could not hear prayer,
 a mouth that could not speak
 and hands that could not help.
But very often
 we select for our gods
 impotent gods such as Baal

and
      we meet with the same type of frustration
      that these prophets met with on the mountain
            that day.
Why,
      in the near,
            as it approached noon,
why,
      in their anxiety,
         they began
         to become frantic.
      And they began
         to cut themselves with stones.
      And they began
         to go through all kinds
         of frantic commotions,
     trying
         to bring Baal around.
But
      as the noon hour
         began to approach,
why,
      the prophet
         Elijah began
         to make fun of them.
      He said, "You better call
         a little louder.
      Maybe your god
         is asleep,
      or maybe he's gone off
         on a journey,
      and maybe even he is deaf
         and unable to hear you.
         You better call a little louder."
O Lord.
      But at high noon,
great God,
      at high noon,
         I heard him say,
         "My time has come.
      I've given you
         the first opportunity

and you've had every chance
      to call on your god
      and prove him to the nation.
But
    miserably
      your god has failed.
Great God.
    Let me build
      my altar now.
O Lord.
    Bring me twelve
      stones
      to represent
      the twelve tribes
      of Israel.
    Bring me a stone
      great God, for Reuben,
    and bring me a stone
      for Judah.
    And bring me a stone
      for Benjamin,
      and I want a stone
for Manasseh.
    And I want a stone
      for all twelve
      of the tribes.
    I want the whole nation
      represented here today.
    And then bring me four barrels of water
      when I build the altar.
    I want to put the water on there
      that nobody will say
      that I'm trying to bring on a trick."
O Lord.
And
    when noon had come
      and when the altar was built,
    he bowed down
      at the altar
    to tell the Lord,
    "O Lord,
    O Lord,

I'm here alone.
There are eight hundred and fifty prophets here
        on the other side,
And Israel has become impotent,
and Israel is hesitant
to speak out for you,
and I'm standing alone today
because I know you live.
O Lord.
        The nations have you on trial today.
Great God.
        If you fail me,
        if you fail me,
        you'll fail Israel today.
O Lord.
        If you fail me,
great God,
        you'll let me down today."
O Lord.
        He kept on praying
        and eventually
        the fire rained down
        and licked up the water
        and licked up the stone,
great God.
Oh yes.
        And here is what I want to say
                in my conclusion today,
        All I want to say to you,
        how long
        will you halt
                between two opinions?
        How long
        will you vacillate
                where God is concerned?
        If money is your god,
                serve money.
        If gold is your god,
                serve gold.
        If popularity is your god,
                serve popularity.
        But if God is your God,

you ought to serve God.
O Lord.
You ought to say, "Lord.
Lord.
Lord.
[?]
I mean to serve him.
God
if you need my hands,
use them.
If you need my life
use it as an instrument."
Ohh!
O Lord.
Great God.
I'm wondering,
I'm wondering,
are you undecided today,
are you undecided tonight,
is God your God?
I want to leave it with you now
that he's mine.
Yes he is.
Ohh!
O Lord.
Ohh, yes.
He's my rock tonight
in a wearied land.
He's my shelter
when I'm outdoors.
Ohh!
O Lord.
Ohh yes,
yes.
I'm wondering,
I'm wondering.

[Speaking:] I'm just wondering. How long will you halt between two opinions? How long will you be undecided? When will you make up your mind that Jehovah God is God and there is no other, there is no other?

5

Dry Bones
in the Valley

[*The Prophet and the Valley of Dry Bones;
From Bones to Destiny*].
Chess LP-36. Recorded mid-1950s.

"The hand of the Lord was upon me, and carried me out in the Spirit of the Lord, and set me down in the midst of the valley which was full of bones, and caused me to pass by them round about: and, behold, there were very many in the open valley; and, lo, they were very dry. And he said unto me, Son of man, can these bones live? And I answered, O Lord God, thou knoweth. And again he said unto me, Prophesy from these bones, and say unto them, O ye dry bones, hear the word of the Lord." [Ezekiel 37:1–4]

The prophet and the valley of dry bones.

Among those who were carried away was a young man by the name of Ezekiel, who had obviously been trained to be a priest. When we study his minute descriptions of the temple order and of the temple liturgy, when we read of his intimate knowledge of things directly or indirectly concerned with Judaism, we must conclude that he had formal training as a priest. But along with the vision that Ezekiel reveals here, along with others that he records in his book, one thing he wanted to convince Israel of [was] that her God had not fallen, and her God was not dead. He wanted Israel to understand that her God, as he depicts in the vision where he saw the vague outlines of a man sitting upon a chariot throne engulfed in a cloud, and with priestly functionaries going in and coming out from the mercy seat, he was saying when he told them about wheels that he saw in the middle of wheels, and that these wheels were guarded by angels, and that these wheels had eyes, and that these wheels did not deviate from their course; he was telling Israel first about the overruling Providence and power of God, and about [how] Israel was a part of God's eternal plans and purposes. While Israel was one wheel, ever moving, and above that was another wheel—that was the Babylonian wheel. It was moving. And that above that was another wheel, which was God's universal wheel and

God's universal plan. And all of these wheels were moving because all of God's plans are always moving. Maybe you think you have stopped them, maybe you think you have blocked them, maybe you can't see the movement. But God's plans never stand still. You can't bother them and you can't stop them. For the writer here tells us that angels were on guard. (Pray with me if you please.)

So to Israel, we see in this vision, Babylon was a desolate place. Babylon represented a valley to Israel, a valley of depravity, a valley of disfranchisement, a valley of hopelessness, a valley of dry bones, a valley of lifelessness. And one of the great cities of the ancient times—Babylon—to Israel was a valley. Someone might marvel if Babylon was a great city how could it be regarded by the Israelites as a valley? Well, you see, a city may be one thing to one people, or a country may mean one thing to one people, and altogether another thing to another people. When the white Europeans came to this country, embarked upon these shores, America to them was a land of promise, was a mountaintop of possibilities, was a mountaintop of adventure. But to the Negro, when he embarked upon these shores, America to him was a valley: a valley of slave huts, a valley of slavery and oppression, a valley of sorrow; so that often we had to sing:

> One of these days, I'm going to eat at the feasting table;
> One of these days, the chariot of God will swing low.

(I wished I had somebody here praying with me.) So that Babylon to Israel was a place of hopelessness. It was a valley of dry bones. A valley of dry bones. Well, the prophet tells it—. And considering a prophet, what is a prophet, anyway, since the prophet was God's representative, God's ambassador, God's watchman there in Babylon? You know, and the word *prophet* can be interchanged with the word *preacher,* for a prophet is a preacher, and a preacher ought to be a prophet. Not a prophet such as we are told and talk about sometime, not a funny person, not somebody with their head tied up or selling luck or anything like that, not that kind of prophet. But I mean a real prophet: a prophet called of God, a prophet born of God, a prophet sent from God, a prophet inspired of God. For a prophet is one who knows the past, who understands the present, and out of his knowledge of the past and his insight of the present, he's able to predict the future. A prophet is one who has sight, insight, and foresight. With sight he looks on things. With insight he looks into things. With foresight he looks beyond things.

Such a man was Ezekiel. And he uses the symbol of a valley to describe Israel's Babylonian situation. They symbol of a valley. For you see, a valley suggests a low place between mountains. And to Israel there were obstructing mountains surrounding her, her situation in Babylon. Economic mountains, social and political mountains, religious mountains encircled and enclosed her in. And she was down here in the stagnant air of a valley in Babylon.

So that he said that he was in the Spirit, and that gives validity to it, you know. People speak a little bit about the Spirit now, but I'm afraid that the church is losing a great deal of its spiritual consciousness. It wasn't unusual for folk to say, when I was growing up as a boy, "The Spirit told me" to do certain things, or "I was led by the Spirit" to do certain things. So that this prophet was a spiritual-minded, a Spirit-filled, God-conscious prophet.

And he said, while being in the Spirit, the Lord led him out to the valley, and then led him to the midst of the valley and sat him down in the midst of it. What he was really saying [was] that God led him to the heart of Israel's problems, and Israel's situation in Babylon. That's what he was saying. God took him in a thoroughgoing survey, in a thoroughgoing analysis and understanding of Israel's Babylonian situation. And when the Lord had led him to the heart of Israel's problems, set him down there, then for fear that way out on the periphery of things he'd miss something, then the Lord led him round and about the valley, or took him and encompassed the valley, circled it on all sides that he might not miss the remotest problems of Israel's situation.

And when the survey was thorough and complete the Lord posed a question to him. "Son of man." I wish you could hear him saying that. "Son of man, can these bones live?" That *son of man* seemed to be reminiscent of man's limitations, reminiscent of man's finiteness, man's humanity. Son of man. Son of man, you are a scholar, you are an educator. Son of man, you are a scientist: Can these bones live? Son of man, you are an engineer: Can these bones live? Son of man, you are a heart specialist; son of man, you are a geologist, you are a botanist, you are a specialist in various phases of the human body, you are a psychologist and psychiatrist, you know all about drives and reactions and responses and tendencies. I want to know with all of this knowledge can you tell me: Can these bones live? Can these bones live? Son of man, you've found pathways in the air. You have circumvented the earth. Son of man, you've found highways upon the sea, and you've made your own highways under the sea: Can these bones live? Can these bones live?

The prophet had to give up. The prophet had to admit his ignorance. The prophet had to admit that he didn't know the answer to the secret of life. Oh, we know a lot of things. We know what the human problems are, we know men are mean, we know men are prejudiced, we know that men are narrow-minded, and we know they are selfish. We know men are unkind, ruthless, and cruel. We know men are murderers and sinful. But what we don't know is what to do about it!

Oh, we know what the problem is. We have made an analysis of it. We have already diagnosed the case, but what we can't do is write a prescription. (I wished I had somebody here praying with me.) So that the prophet had to say, "Lord, thou knoweth. Lord, thou knoweth." When it came to the answer of many of life's perplexing problems, when it comes to a solution to these problems, Lord, thou knoweth. I submit myself before you: limited, finite, ignorant and helpless, like dry bones in a valley, and thou knoweth, thou hath the answer. And you know there's one thing about God, when we go to him sincerely, when we have been overwhelmed by some problem that we are unable to grapple with, put it at his feet; ultimately, if we have faith, he'll give us the answer. He'll work it out for us.

And Ezekiel declared that he didn't know, and it was in the hands of God to give the answer. [Whooping:]

Why,
  the Lord,
  after Ezekiel had
  surveyed
and
  had gotten a full understanding
    of what the Babylonian problem was,
why,
  he said to him,
why,
  "You go out
  if you want the answer,
  and preach to those dry bones."
  "Well, Lord,
  it looks like a,
  a helpless thing,
  it looks like an unprofitable thing,
  for me to go out
    and preach to dry bones.
  Some of the living souls
    that
  I preach to
    don't respond to me,
and
  what could I expect
    from dry bones?"
  But the Lord urged him
  to go on out
    and preach anyhow.
  You know,

God's ways,
    you know,
are above man's ways.

And

    you can't always understand
        why
        he orders you to do certain things.
But if the Lord orders you,
        go on anyhow.

Why,

    you may not see it,
        but there is a way.
You may not know what you're doing,
        but God has it worked out.
(I don't believe you know what I'm talking about.)

O Lord.

    And I saw that man
        go out in that valley,
    in that valley
        of dry bones,
        of dry bones,

o Lord,

    and stood there,

and

    preached to those dry bones.
You know the Lord had given him
        a text to preach on.

Well,

    "Lord, what can I preach
        to dry bones about?

O Lord.

    Lord, what kind of subject
        and what kind of text
        can I use?"

O Lord.

    "Just go there,
        and use this text:
    tell those dry bones
        to hear the word of the Lord,
        to hear the word of the Lord."

O Lord.

    I'm sure

it must have been discouraging sometime
for him to stand there
day and night
and preach in that valley
of dry bones,
to preach in that valley of helplessness
and in that valley
of lifelessness,
in that valley
of hopelessness,

my Lord,

to stand there and preach
and not be able to see
what the results would be,

o Lord,

but he preached on anyhow.

Oh yes.

And then one morning
the valley began to rumble,

yes it did.

One morning
the valley began to shake,

and

there was a mighty
moving around.

O Lord.

Then one morning,
yes,
when he looked around
to observe this rumbling,

great God,

he saw the old dry bones
in motion.

Yes.

Foot bone
was searching out an
ankle bone.

O Lord.

And ankle bone
was moving on toward
knee bone.

Oh yes.

And knee bone
    was connecting with thigh bones.
And thigh bones
    were moving on toward hip bones.
And

hip bones
were moving toward back bones,
    yes they were.
And back bone
was joining on to shoulder bone.
And shoulder bone
was tying in with neck bone.
And neck bone
    was turning to head bone.
O Lord.

The prophet kept on preaching,
    yes he did,
    kept on preaching,
"Oh ye dry bones
    hear the word of the Lord."
O Lord.

And the Lord said, "Wait a minute now.
    I want you to preach on a new theme.
Yes.

I want you
to just wait a little while
and let me extract matter
    from the universe.
Yes.

And let me order that matter
to come together
and form man's anatomy.
Let flesh get on the bone.
Let skin
    begin to cover those skeletons."
O Lord.

"But Lord,
all we have now
    are corpses here
    lying on the ground."
"Turn now
    and preach to the wind.

Tell the wind
     that God wants the wind to blow,"
Lord God,
"and blow breath into these bodies."
My Lord.
    "Tell those bones,
    'Hear my words.' "
And that's my solution tonight,
that's my answer tonight
to every problem that we have:
that is to hear God's words.
Hear God's words.
It's all right
     to go to the United Nations,
it's all right
     to preach on international fellowship,
it's all right
     to call on the scholars,
     to call on our businessmen,
      it's all right,
but I tell you what you had better do:
hear God's words,
hear God's words.
His words!
His words.
His word.
His word
is a bridge in deep water.
His word
is a lamp to your stumbling feet,
yes it is.
    His word,
        oh his word.
Great God.
    God's words.
    Oh
        his words
will bring peace
     into every confused heart;
his words
     will bring order
     in every disorderly life;

his words
　　　will lift up and raise men up.
Yes they will.
　　His words,
　　oh, his word,
　　ohh,
　　oh, God's words.
　　God's word.
　　God's words.
　　God's word
　　　　is still my answer.

[Singing:]
　　Heaven and earth may pass away,
　　but his word will always stand.
　　Always stand.
　　Always stand.
　　I'm trying to live on his words.
　　And one of these mornings when troubles are over,
　　and when trials are ended,
　　when I get over to the Jordan,
　　I want his Word right there.
　　Right there,
　　right there.
　　I want him to let his Word
　　be shaped like a vessel
　　and let my soul
　　ohh
　　step on over.
　　Here's my life.
　　Is anybody here tonight
　　that knows anything about God's words?
　　I have
　　his words
　　way down in my heart,
　　and, and, and, Lord,
　　I'm still counting on his Word,
　　I'm still leaning and leaning,
　　and I'm still waiting
　　and watching for his words.

6

Without a Song

Chess LP-52.
Recorded mid-1950s.

. . . One hundred and thirty-seventh Psalm, the first four verses will be the basis of our discussion. "By the rivers of Babylon, there we set down, yea, we wept when we remembered Zion. We hanged our harps upon the willows in the midst thereof, for they that carried us away captive required of us a song; and they that wasted us required of us mirth, saying, Sing us one of the songs of Zion. How shall we sing the Lord's song in a strange land?"

The subject that we're using tonight is, Without a song. Without a song.

Here they were, these proud Hebrews, in Babylon, some of whom had been courtiers, government officials, rabbis, teachers, scholars, leaders in intellectual and religious thought, leaders in philosophical thought, sages. Here they were, prisoners of war, forced to reside in a strange, pagan land. Their conquerors posed a request. Said they, when they had sufficiently observed these Hebrews, had appraised them for what they were, knew them to be scholars and experts in political science, and priests and thinkers, but the Babylonians had all of these things themselves. They had their scholars, they had their astrologers, they had their scientists, they had their philosophers. They had built up a credible government. They had the great court of Hammurabi's that they could boast of, the wisdom of which has survived all the ages, and they weren't particularly worried about the Jews along that line. But what they were concerned about was, is getting them to do something that they really did appreciate. They possessed the ability to do something that they regarded to be unique. And so they petitioned them. Said they, "Sing us one of Zion's songs." (I wish you'd pray with me just a little while.) "Sing for us one of Zion's songs." Now the Jews, or the Hebrews, refused. They refused on the grounds that they didn't think that the request and its fulfillment would be timely. They thought that it would be a bit disorderly and out of place, and so they refused this Babylonian request. Said they, "How can we sing the songs of Zion in a strange land?"

I take the position that they should have sung. Yes, they were in a strange land; yes, they were among so-called heathens; yes, the situation in which they found themselves was an unfamiliar situation and possibly was not conducive to inspire them into spiritual expression. But even under adverse circumstances, you ought to sing sometimes. And not only sing, sing some of Zion's songs. (I don't believe you know what I'm talking about.)

You see, there is something universal about singing, something that has in it a universal appeal. Sometimes you don't have to know what the words of the singer may be, but you appreciate the melody and the music of the song. It has a universal appeal. And singing can do a lot of things for you. Many messages can be conveyed through a song. You see, we have patriotic songs when we want to express our loyalty and devotion to land and country. We have songs of valor and bravery. Then we have songs of happiness, and then songs of sadness. We have songs of confusion and trial, burden and tribulation. Then we have songs of peace and a brighter day. We have songs of promise, we have songs of God and destiny. We have songs of life and death. So that any message that you really want to get over, you can get it over in a song. Isn't it so?

I notice that some of the West Indians in one of the British possessions, some of the inhabitants of the country, adopted the practice of campaigning for office through songs. What they couldn't get up on the stage and say, they could sing. So it's true with singing sometimes. Some things you can't say, you can sing. Isn't it so? So I think the Jews, or the Hebrews, should have sung, in that strange land, in that strange land.

It is said that Roland Hayes on one occasion went to Berlin, Germany, to sing in one of the great and celebrated music houses of Berlin. At the time, Nazism was arising, and some of them did not want this Georgia Negro to come and stand on the stage where their great immortals had stood, and sing. It is said that on the day of the concert and about the time that Roland Hayes was to go on stage, his handlers and his attendants took him to the rear of the building and spirited him in, and then when they called for him, he walked out on the stage. And when he walked out on the stage, those who resented him and those who opposed him went into howls and hisses to make it impossible for him to sing. He stood there for a long time with his eyes closed and his arms folded, and then when apparently the noise would not subside, he just kept his eyes closed and his arms folded, and began singing in that great tenor voice, "Lord, thou art my peace, thou art my peace." And that great voice began to rise and soar above the noise, and search that great building, and then hisser and howler after howler began to get quiet and listen to that great voice. Eventually the whole house became quiet and listened, listened, and was moved and thrilled and inspired by this great artist. And when he had finished, that same crowd that intended to make it impossible for him to sing, many of them ran to the stage and took him upon their shoulders and marched down the aisle, hailing and acclaiming him. I'm trying to tell you what can be done in a song. (I don't believe you know what I'm talking about.) "Thou art my peace."

Why, take for example, as I come toward the close, the Negro found himself in a similar situation during his slave experiences, and frequently he was called upon to sing. And he always complied, he never missed a chance to sing, because it was his songs and the gospel that he heard by those ancient ministers that kept hope alive in his heart. I think they should have sung.

The story is told by Dr. Miles Mark Fisher about an old woman, either in the Carolinas or in Georgia, in those days when a great English preacher, the brother of John Wesley, came over to preach. Many of the Negroes wanted to see this great preacher. Frequently they could sit in the church, at least in the balcony, if the balcony was not crowded, if most of the regular members were on the main floor. But on this particular occasion the place was packed, and they stood on the outside, looking through the window, listening at this English preacher preach the gospel. And when the sermon was over and the invitation was extended, one old lady walked in the front door, and walked down the aisle, and took the seat to join the church. Pastor came up and said, "Lady, you can't join this church." She said, "But sir, I got 'eligion. I've been converted. I felt the power of God here today while the man preached, and I want to jine the church." He said, "But you can't join this church. Go and join some other church, some of your own churches." And when he insisted that she could not join, she went on down the aisle, mumbling to herself, saying, "I'm going to tell God one of these days how you treat me," as tears rolled down her cheeks.

It is said that those who were looking in the window began to sing a song. As the old lady's name was Mary, they sang,

> Oh Mary, don't weep, don't mourn;
> Pharaoh's army got drownded;
> Mary, don't weep, and then don't mourn.

Think of the message that is wrapped up in that song. I think that everybody ought to have a song. I think that Israel should have sung down in Babylon. (I don't believe you know what I'm talking about.)

It is said that during the slave experiences, showing on the other hand where the Negroes took just the other position, as compared with the Hebrews, in their oppression. It is said that many times when they had no suits, that their clothes were made out of the cotton sacks that they put the cotton in, a straight, long garment, and very often when they could not eat the meal or the food that they prepared for their masters, many times corn mush was boiled and placed in troughs and they were made to eat that, while they had served a banquet table that was full of delicacies and the finest foods. But he didn't grow disheartened and he didn't lose hope. He began singing: "I'm going to put on a long, white robe, one of these days." I can't do it now, but one of these days. And though I eat from troughs now, and my meal may be rough and of the poorest kind, and completely stripped of vitamins, etcetera, but one of these days I'm going to set at the feasting table, one of these days. Though I have no shoes to wear now, I have no shoes to wear now, I must go bare of foot now, but one of these days I'm going to put on my golden slippers one of these days. Oh yes, I must work from sun to sun—(I don't believe you know what I'm talking about)—and I must do the hardest labor, without even a thought of compensation for my toil, but I'm going to rest and not get tired one of these days. (I wish you knew what I was talking about.)

I'm trying to tell you that the Negro sang. Through his darkness, through his trials, and through his tribulations, he sang. It is said that very often, when he had no thought of ever having a chance to ride in one of the great chariots or surreys that he saw his bosses riding around in, he dreamed of a day—no wonder somebody said, "You can't keep me from dreaming, and you can't keep me from singing." Isn't it so? He stood in the fields of Georgia, of Alabama and Tennessee, in the Virginias and other places, and he saw them gliding along, merrily and comfortably, and he dreamed, and then sang:

> Swing low, sweet chariot,
> coming for to carry me home.

I can't ride in a chariot now, my situation prevents me from riding now, but one of these days, a chariot is going to swing low for me. (I don't believe you know what I'm talking about.)

And very often, when he was forbidden to congregate, not so much on the basis, or on the grounds that the bosses were antireligious or didn't want them to engage in religion, but they feared that this congregating would create unity and give rise to thoughts of liberation, and so they forbade them, in many cases, to congregate. But very often one of the trusted ones would decide on a place where they were going to meet under the shade of the night, and the password was, as he went from one slave hut to another,

> Steal away, steal away to Jesus.
> We ain't got long to stay here.

(I don't believe you know what I'm talking about.) I think that we ought to sing, no matter how troublesome our situations become, no matter how trying our situations become. I think we ought to sing. You see, Israel had not grown universal-minded at this time. She was still hampered by her nationalistic thinking. She was still hampered by many inhibitions that were inherent in their culture, and they wouldn't sing. But I'm sure they could have done a lot for Babylon if they had sung. I'm sure that Babylon would have been better off if they had heard that Israel's God was the God that created the world, that scooped out the seas with the palm of his hand, and who held the waters, as it were, in the skirts of his garments. I'm sure Babylon would have been helped to know that Israel's God was a God who loved his people, who not only loved his people but who looked out for them, and who made ways for them.

And those of you who know our God tonight, know that he will make a way. And you know, people have ways of segregating certain communities and segregating certain peoples, and who act like their religion is too good to go certain places. But thank God that as I think on the life of Jesus, there was no place that our God and our Christ would not go: in the harlots' homes, in the publicans' homes, in sinners' homes, wherever people were, our Christ and our Lord and master went there. And not only did he go there, he did things after he went there.   [Whooping:]

And
   I want to tell you tonight
     that's listening to me,
why,
   when you've got so much religion
     that you can't mingle with people,
and
   that you're afraid
     of certain people,
   let me tell you,
     you've got too much religion.
   Sometimes
   you can't reach some people
     without coming close to them.
O Lord.
   You have to get near them
     and let them understand you,
and
   tell them
     that God loves them
and that
   not only does God love them
     but let them know that you love them also

You can't
reach people
if they don't believe
that you're interested in them.
If they don't believe
that you love them,
and that you're concerned about them,
if you give them the impression
that you feel
that you're better than they are,
I doubt
whether you'll ever be able to reach them.
O Lord.
And I don't think
that the Lord intended for it to be that way anyhow.
If you're good,
and if you're satisfied,
if you've dug deep,
and sounded well,
if you've got your house
on a solid rock,
you ought to could trust your religion
anywhere.
Isn't it so?
O Lord.
If your religion
can't
carry you by the bar,
you don't have too much anyway.
(I don't believe you know what I'm talking about tonight.)
O Lord.
If your religion
won't hold you
when you come face to face
with temptation,
great God,
my Lord,
you don't have enough anyway,
and you need to try it out
and see what it'll do anyhow.
O Lord.
If you don't know
whether you are strong or not,

you ought to test yourself sometime.
(I don't believe you know what I mean tonight.)
Anyway,
I'm going to sing the songs of Zion.
O Lord.
     I know the time
          when people didn't mind singing them
          at home,
          in the streets,
          in the field,
          anywhere.
O Lord.
     Early in the morning
          you could hear some old child of God,
o Lord,
     whose voice
          would ride the morning air,
          sing,
     "I love the Lord,
          he heard my cry,
          and then pitied every groan.
Yes,
     long as I live,
          while trouble rise,
          I'll hasten to his throne."
O Lord.
     You could hear him out across the field early
          in the morning saying,
yes,
o Lord,
why,
     "On Jordan's
          stormy banks I stand,
          and cast a wishful eye,
    to Canaan's fair
          and happy land,
          and where my mother shall lie."
O Lord.
     I can hear them saying,
     "Amazing grace,
          how sweet the sound,
          that saved a wretch like me.
     I once was lost,

> but now am found,
> was blind but now I see."

O Lord.

> You ought to sing.
> Every heart
> ought to have a song,
> and every lip
> ought to proclaim
> the goodness of God
> by way of song.

O Lord.

> I don't want to lose my song,
> and I don't want to be in that crowd
> that's without a song.

O Lord.

> I want to sing,
> and in my song,
> tell people
> that he's a way-provider,
> and that my God is a way-maker.

O Lord.

> Everywhere,
> everywhere,
> everywhere,
> everywhere I go,
> I want to let the world know
> through my song,
> that he's a lamp
> in a dark place,

o Lord.

> Everywhere,
> everywhere,
> everywhere,
> everywhere I go,
> every,
> ah everywhere I go,
> I want to let the world know
> that when I'm a lost sheep,
> my Lord is a shepherd,
> and he holds my hand,
> through my song.
> I want to keep on singing,

great God,
>I want to keep on singing,
>>until somebody knows,

yes,
>that my rock in a wearied land,
>is salvation
>>to every lost soul.

O Lord.
>Everywhere,
>>everywhere,
>ah everywhere,
>(I don't believe you know what I mean,)
>oh everywhere,
>>I said everywhere I go,
>every,
>>yes,
>ah everywhere,
>>I said everywhere
>ohh!
>>yes.
>Maybe you don't know what I'm talking about.
>I'm going to keep on singing,

yes I am.
>Ohh!
>I said everywhere I go,
>I'm going to hold on to my song
>>and keep on singing it.

Yes I am.
>Ohh!
>Ohh yes,
>yes.
>Ohh yes,
>Ohh yes,
>Did you know [?]
>Are you going to sing on?
>>Lord, God.
>Do you have a song in your heart?

And,
o Lord,
>ohh yes,
>ohh yes,
>ohh yes!

7

Jacob Wrestling the Angel

Chess LP-22.
Recorded mid-1950s.

In the book of Genesis, from about the thirtieth chapter and several of the following chapters, and read the entire life of this biblical character, and of this, one of the fathers of the nation of Israel. I think that there is something about his life that we would do well to think about. I elected to do this upon talking with a few people recently, many of whom are well-known people and high churchmen, some of them, not necessarily preachers, but leading churchmen and women who do not even know a Bible story. Hmm? And that is pathetic, isn't it? No wonder we have so much trouble with folk in church: they know so little about it, so little not only about the church but of the Bible of the church.

First of all, Jacob stands out in Hebrew history, as I have previously suggested, as one of the fathers of the nation. He is venerated and esteemed today for his contribution to Israel as a nation. He made contributions not only to the religious experience of Israel as a nation, but several basic things about the national and political life of the nation were originated, according to the record, by Jacob. And much about him and his personality, his views, his thinking, have been preserved down through the centuries by this peculiar people.

The first thing I want you to think about Jacob is that he had an early vision of God. An early vision of God. Now this is not to say that Jacob was not strictly human, because he was. He was very human. In a lot of respects too human, for although he had a vision of God, there were a lot of things about him in his earlier life that he would have done well to have gotten rid of immediately. For his very name suggests a trickster, a deceiver, a supplanter, you understand, a man of extreme selfishness and self-centeredness.

Well, I think that we can cite a few incidents that will set that fact apart. And that is, from the early childhood of this young man who finally became a giant in the history of the nation and a stalwart and a champion of Israelitic cause, he was selfish to the point where he contemplated continuously and connived and conspired how he could trick his own brother out of his birthright. And not only his birthright, but to succeed his father as the priest and leader of the family. But along with that went a blessing that was usually bequeathed by the father. So Jacob was not content to trick his brother and get the birthright, but also he wanted the blessing that his father gave, finally to the eldest son. And of course when he saw his brother, when he found him at his weakest point, when he found him available for attack, hungry and faint, he made him swear and pledge that he would relinquish all claims to the birthright and turn it over to him.

And then in league with his mother, when his father decided that the sun of life was sinking low, time was plowing furrows in his face, and his eyes had grown weary of seeing, and his body was bending under the weight of many years, he said, "Now, my son, go out and bring me some of the dishes that you usually kill the wild game and prepare for me. And let me give you the blessing before I die." Mother said, "Get busy, now." Said to Jacob, her favorite, "Get busy, your daddy's planning to give out that blessing today, you come in and get it. I'm going to disguise you and make you hairy like your brother and I'm going to fix you up [so] that you can trick your father." And you know the story of how he came by it, when his brother returned after the father had given the blessing, when his brother returned and found a new trick that had been pulled on him, he became angry and he had to leave home.

But you know there are a lot of Jacobs around yet. All of them are not dead. It's some more tricksters are around, it's some more double-crossers around, some more deceivers around. There are some more people who feel that they can live off their wits by taking advantage of other people. But as I said today, the thing that was outstanding about the Joseph story is true also in relation to the Jacob story. To dedicate oneself to the highest good that he knows, to hold on to the highest ideals that he knows, and to never compromise certain principles—reward and victory and success may be slow for you, but victory is surely yours if you do not allow your spirit, your ambition, your faith to be destroyed under the impact of these trials and crises. Jacob got into a lot of things that he could have avoided but for the fact that he himself was always practicing trickery. And I want you to understand when you set out in life to take advantage of people, ultimately you're going to be found out, and people will start dealing with you as you deal with people. (I wonder if you know what I'm talking about tonight?)

And so, one night on his way to his uncle's home, one night leaving Canaan en route to Assyria, one night while traveling upon the desert alone, feeling condemned and feeling that he had done wrong—because if one has any conception of God he cannot mistreat his brother without feeling it and knowing it and realizing it and being condemned by it himself (pray with me if you please)—he lay down. And obviously he was not acquainted with the omnipresence of God. Obviously he did not understand that God was everywhere. He had a dream that night while his head was lying on a rock, that he saw a ladder that extended from heaven to earth, and that angels were ascending and descending up and down that ladder to where he was. And when he awakened he became afraid, he said, "This is an awful place, this must be the gates of heaven. Surely the Lord is in this place and I knew it not. Now, Lord, since I know you're here, and I know that you know what I've done, and I know you understand why I'm out here alone, I'd like to enter into a covenant with you. I'm alone, I'm away from home, I can't go back soon, my brother is out to get me. If you take care of me while I'm gone, if you'd keep me in the way that I'd go, if you'd protect me, a tenth of all that I get a hold to I'll give back to you."

But you see, one experience apparently is not enough to strip us of those things that we find ourselves shedding as we go up through life. Jacob didn't stop simply because he had this early vision of God. He was still a little tricky. He got down there with his uncle, you know. Of course, his uncle was tricky with him! And his uncle, after making him marry the oldest daughter first, said, now, Jacob said, "Well, it's time to be getting out on my own." His uncle said, "Well, I need you, you've been a blessing to me since you've been here, it seems like some kind of deal could be worked out where you could stay with me a little longer." Jacob, being conniving, he said, "Well, now, I'll tell you what you do. If you will—this will be my wages, if you will just give me all the spotted cows. You know you don't have many spotted cows in your herd. If you just give me all the spotted cows, I will accept that as just compensation for my services."

But Jacob wasn't contented to simply let time and nature take its course with the spotted cows. He found some branches, green branches, and trimmed rings around them, stripes around them, and put those striped sticks in the water where the cows had to drink, designed obviously to influence the conception of those cows and create more spotted cattle in his uncle's herd. Then one day when he had enough, he decided after the old man left he'd get everything and get both of his daughters, and all of his children and get all of his spotted cattle and leave in the absence of the old man. The old man came and found that he had taken up root and branch and left. He set out after him. But having caught up with him, he decided, Well, the boy has been with me for fourteen years and a little longer, he is my son-in-law, he's married to two of my daughters, and all of these children are my grandchildren, so I can't hurt him. I guess I'll have to compromise with him. I'll tell him what we'll do: "Let's set up here a little memorial of the dissolution of this grievance.

This stone will be a memorial to our compromise and may the Lord watch between me and thee when we are absent one from another."

But you see, there is a danger. There is a danger. You see, you may get away, you may get by, being a trickster, but ultimately your tricks will catch up with you. I say you may get by, but you haven't gotten away. Now he'd run away from Esau and he'd gotten off from the vineyards of his father-in-law, but you see, his past was catching up with him. He was ready to go back home and he couldn't get back home without meeting up and accounting with Esau. And so this night, as he approached the banks of Jabbok, out there near a mountainside called Peniel, he decided to tell his servants, "I want you to ride on ahead of me, and tell my brother I'm on my way home. I'd like to come home. Tell him I've been successful, that I have many camels, many sheep, many goats, and I went across the brook here with only my staff, but I'm on my way back with two bands. Tell him that. And I'm willing to settle up with him." But the servant came running back saying, "Master, your brother is on his way to meet you with four hundred men. But he hasn't given me any word of consolation to you."

And so, my brothers and sisters, Jacob realized now the haunts and experiences of the past were crowding in on him, realized now some of the battles that he had ducked in the past he had to face now. He realized now the challenge of life was looming up in the personality of his brother. He had to meet his brother. And so he organized his servants in one band, with his cattle in front of them, and then his handmaidens in another group, and his wife Leah in another group behind them, and Rachel and his son Joseph behind her, and her children, and decided to put all of these between him and his brother, to put all of these between him and his past.   [Whooping:]

But my brothers and sisters,
why,
if you have not dealt
squarely and faithfully
in life,
if your dealings have not been honest,
somewhere along the line life demands
that you must pay off
and that you must reckon one way or another.
O Lord.
And so the ghost of the past
was crowding in
on Jacob.
And
when he organized all of these bands

                    between him
                    and the fury
                    and vengeance of his brother,
            he went on over
                    to this mountainside
and
            said, "Now Lord
                    I know I've done wrong,
            I'm going to be out here
                    all night long,
yes,
            my children
                    are out there on
                    across the brook;
and
            my wife and family
                    are on the other side,
            and I've delayed
                    my crossing
                    to talk with you
                    before the sunrise in the morning
                    and before I meet my brother,
            for tomorrow
                    I must come face to face
                    with Esau.
O Lord.
            Now I know
                    I must face myself.
O Lord.
            I've been avoiding this
                    a long time,
and
            I've been compromising
                    with myself a long time.
            I've been creating excuses
                    for myself a long time.
            I've been refusing to look myself
                    squarely in the face
                    a long time.
            But now I know
                    the time has come.
O Lord.

I've deceived my brother,
    I've deceived my father,

and

I've double-crossed my uncle,
    and I've done wrong
    with everybody that I came in contact.

O Lord.

I'm getting older now,
    and I have wives and children.

O Lord.

I realize now
    that if I'm ever going to straighten up,
    I've got to do it now.

Oh yes.

And Lord I know—"
(You ought to read the prayer sometime
    as you read this passage.)
"I'm not deserving," he said,
    "of the least of all your blessings,
    no I'm not,

O Lord,

but Lord please,
    Lord please."
Can't you envisage him out there
    on that dark mountainside,
    that night a-wrestling with the angel.

O Lord.

You know when you read
    about Jacob wrestling with that angel,
for Jacob
was wrestling with Jacob as much
    as he was wrestling with an angel,

yes he was.

He was wrestling with himself,
he was wrestling with his conscience,
he was wrestling with his disposition,
he was wrestling with his character,

yes he was.

O Lord.

But all night long—
(I'm going to let this alone directly.
It's a little too hot for this.)

all night long,
all night long,
        he took an inventory,
all night long,
        he turned his heart as it were,
        outside in,
all night long,
        he examined his character
        and his disposition,
all night long,
he laid himself bare
        before God,
        yes he did.
O Lord.
        But Jacob said early in the morning
        when he wouldn't give up
                the angel blessed him
                and changed his name
                and told him his name would no more be Jacob
                which signaled a symbol of a trickster,
                but his new name would be Israel,
                a prince of power
                with both God and man.
O Lord.
        And I want to say to you tonight
                in my conclusion,
                you ought to finish yourselves,
                yes you should.
        There are a lot of things about us all
                that we ought to look at.
        There are a lot of things about us all
                that we ought to face.
        There are a lot of things about us all
                that we ought to admit.
O Lord.
        You know there are wrong things about us all
                that we do not admit even to ourselves,
                we ought to face ourselves.
        One night you ought to get down
                on your knees,
        on the lonely mountainside
                of prayer,

and talk to God about yourself.
O Lord.
Wrestle with him
all night long,
wrestle with him,
struggle with him,
struggle with the demon
that's in you,
struggle with all of those evil spirits
that are within you.
O Lord.
Tell the Lord,
just tell the Lord,
ohh
tell the Lord,
ohh
just tell the Lord,
ohh
tell the Lord,
"I want to be a better child,
I know I've been wrong,
I know I've even thought wrong,
I know my whole outlook on life was wrong,
but o Lord,
ohh,
o Lord,
o Lord,
o Lord,
o Lord,
I want to be a better child,
yes.
Make me
strong where I'm weak,
prop me
up where I'm leaning,
yes,
build me up
where I've been torn down,
yes,
o Lord,
Lord,
yes,

Lord,
Lord, here's my life,
Lord, here's my heart,
Lord,
      here's my all.
Yes,
      yes,
here's my all.
Make out of me what you want me to be,
Lord, Lord,
Ohh."
(I wish I had somebody here praying with me tonight.)
Ohh,
      yes,
If we'll go to him
      and really face yourself,
he'll make everything all right,
yes he will.
Yes.
Oh yes.
Ohh yes.
Ohh yes.
Yes.
He'll make everything all right.
He'll make everything all right.

8

Moses at the Red Sea

[*Facing a Crisis with God*].
Chess LP-19.
Recorded ca. mid-1950s.

"And the Lord said unto Moses, Wherefore crieth thou unto me? Speak unto the children of Israel, that they go forward: but lift thou up thy hand, and stretch out thine hand over the seas, and divide it: and the children of Israel shall go on dry ground through the midst of the sea." [Exodus 14:15–16]

Facing a crisis with God. Facing a crisis with God.

This particular text has to do with that period in Israel's history when she was marching toward nationhood. God had a destiny for Israel, God had a role in history for Israel to play. Abraham had declared that God had committed himself to make of his seed a great nation. It is interesting to watch how God does things, isn't it? It may seem sometimes that the plans of God are bogged down. It may seem sometime that his plans are blocked and hindered for good, but he always has a way of going through with his plans and seeing them through.

Israel had become the subjects of Egypt, and in accordance with God's purposes and plans Israel was growing rapidly, numerically as a people. So rapid was their growth as a race of people that the Egyptians became fearful and regarded them as a menace to their national security. The result was that the king issued a decree that this nation in their midst should be curbed, violently curbed, and that all of the male children born should be put to death in order to make Egyptian control definite and complete. But you know God always has his Moseses on hand. In every crisis God raises up a Moses. His name may not be Moses but the character of the role that he plays is always the same. His name may be Moses or his name may be Joshua or his name may be David, or his name, you understand, may be Abraham Lincoln or Frederick Douglass or George Washington Carver, but in every crisis God raises up a Moses, especially where the destiny of his people is concerned. You may have a decree out, feeling that you have everything well taken care of, but God can work despite your plans.

Let's take, for example, the case of Moses and the situation under which he was born. God had decreed that certain things that he would do for Israel. Now here's what God did. Right in the face of Pharaoh's decree, he raised Moses right up and then placed him out, or had him placed out, on the bosom of the Nile, and made the liquid Nile become his cradle, and had his sister to watch over him and wouldn't allow a single crocodile to touch him. (I don't believe you're praying with me.) For he was God's Moses. He was God's Moses. And that isn't all God will do. To show you his eternal defiance of those who would obstruct his plans, he touched Pharaoh's daughter's heart, the daughter of the man who issued the decree, and melted her heart in the interest of Moses and made her adopt the very child who had already been decreed to be put to death. That isn't all God did. God made Pharaoh provide a home for him in the palace. (You don't know what I'm talking about.) And then God made Pharaoh take care of him, and God made Pharaoh educate him, and prepare him for the role that history and God had decreed for him. Yes he did. But when his education, his training for political administration and for the role of a legislator and an emancipator, when all of that graduate work had been done, God wasn't through with him. He needed some postgraduate work in religion and he juggled situations and circumstances around and made him restless and stirred the nest and made him get out of Egypt and go over to Midian to sit for awhile at the feet of Jethro and learn religion and learn leadership. (Pray with me if you please.) And in due time one day on a desert the Lord called him, wrapped himself in a bush in the garbs of an apparent flame, and called him, and gave him assurance that he was with him, and then sent him to Pharaoh's court to plead the cause of Israel.

You know the difficulty that he went through in securing the liberty of these people. All of the difficulties were not on Pharaoh's part because sometimes some people can become so adjusted to slavery and oppression they are not willing to give it up. If you'll read the history of this exodus of these people, every time they ran into difficulty on the road to nationhood, they looked back toward the fleshpots and the disfranchisement of Egypt.

But we are concerned primarily about an incident that occurred in the wake of their immediate deliverance from Egypt. They were now at the Red Sea. On the way they had been singing Moses' praises. They saw visions of prosperity. They were not experienced enough to understand that any people who traveled the high road to security, to justice, to all of the privileges that come to citizens, must pay the price. They were not aware, as they traveled, of this cost that entailed. Everybody wants justice, everybody wants freedom, everybody wants what's coming to them, but very few of us take time to think about the price that must be paid for these things and the responsibility that goes along with the achievement of them. Yes, it's beautiful to embrace all these great ideals and these great privileges, but we must carry along with that the costs, the price, the suffering and the sacrifice. (I don't believe you know what I'm talking about.)

And here they were, standing now on the brinks of the Red Sea. Here they were; when they looked behind them, they heard the rattling of the chariot wheels of Pharaoh, who had regretted his decree of deliverance and decided to recapture them and lead them back into the oppression of Egypt. When they looked on either side, mountains prevented their escape. When they looked before them, the Red Sea and its peril loomed large before their imaginations. (I don't believe you know what I'm talking about.) And the same folk who had praised Moses for his valor and for his bravery, for his courage, for his insight, for his great victory of deliverance, began to complain. And Moses said to them, "Stand still and see the salvation of the Lord." (I don't believe you know what I'm talking about.) Stand still. Sometimes, you know, we can get in not only our own way and everybody else's way, but it seems sometime we can get in God's way. Stand still. My God. I heard him say, "The thing that you need is in your hands." (I don't believe you know what I'm talking about.) "The instrument of deliverance is within your hands, it's within your possession. The way out, the powers that need to be brought into exertion, is within you." Good God. "What are you crying about, Moses? What are you looking for? What do you think that you want? Why, the rod of your deliverance is in your own hands. Stretch out the rod that's in your hands. I don't have a new rod to give you, I don't have a new instrument to give you, I don't have a new suggestion for you, I do not have a new plan. Your course has already been charted by destiny. Stretch out the rod that's in your hand." (I don't believe you know what I'm talking about.)

What am I saying? I'm saying that sometimes in the midst of our own crises, in the midst of our own life-problems, in the midst of the things that we find ourselves involved in, sometimes the power of our deliverance is in our own power and in our own possession. What you need, my brothers and sisters, is within you. First of all, it's faith in God, and second, faith in yourself, and thirdly the will and determination to put these into practice. The man who stands and simply cries will never go over his Red Seas. The man who stands or the woman who simply stands and complains, stands before your Red Seas or your own problems, and simply cries, will never find the way out. Did you know, brothers and sisters, that most of the people who have scaled the heights, most of the people who have climbed the mountains in their lives, most of the people who've gone through the valleys of their lives, have not been people who were contented to just stand, just stand. [Whooping:]

Why
            most of them
                        had tried a number of things
                        that they discovered ultimately
                        failed on them.
Why
            most of them that reached outside of themselves,
            and out here among their friends,
                        and among other things
                        to find the solution to their problems,
                        and found themselves
                        in the midst of failure.
O Lord.
            But if you would succeed
                        and really succeed,
            you've got to set down
                        and take count of your own self,
            and set down
                        and appraise your situation.
            Set down
                        and count the cost.
            Set down
and
            realize
                        what is involved.
            Get on your knees
                        and tell God,
            "Everything else I've tried
                        has failed.
            But this is my Red Sea.
O Lord.
And
            you told me
            that what I had in my hand
                        or whatever I have in my life,
                        to stretch it out.
O Lord.
            I don't know what you're going to do,
                        but I'm going to stretch it out.
O Lord.
            I don't know the way
            that you're going to make for me,

but I'm going to do what you tell me to do.
O Lord.
If I fail,
I'm going to fail trying."
(I don't believe you know what I'm talking about tonight.)
O Lord.
(Listen if you please.)
Great God.
Moses,
yes,
wiped his eyes
and
consoled his heart,
yes he did,
and raised his rod
that he had in his hand,
and stretched it out
over the Red Sea.
O Lord.
The God that told him to do that,
why,
had brought Pharaoh down
in his courts.
And
the God that told him to do that
had brought the,
the magicians of Egypt
to be his footstool.
Yes he had.
And now the Lord said,
"Hold out your rod
over the sea."
O Lord.
And listen!
When you exert the powers
that God has given you,
when you go to your extremity
you'll find God waiting for you.
O Lord.
Yes.
To Israel's utter surprise,
the waters of the sea

            began to bank up on one side
            and then bank up on the other.
O Lord.
            And God grabbed
            an east wind
            and fanned the bottom of the Red Sea
            and made the ground dry
            and let them walk across
                    dry ———.
O Lord.
            Let me close
                    when I tell you this.
            There're going to be Red Seas
                    in your life.
            You're going to meet
                    your Pharaohs
                    along life's rugged pathway.
O Lord.
            You're going to be pursued
                    by your enemies.
            O Lord.
            But oh,
                    just wait a little while,
                    and God will make a way.
            He will make a way.
And
            he's always
                    made a way,
            and he's still in the business
                    right now.
            He'll make a way
                    right now.
O Lord.
            Have you examined yourself?
And
            have you realized what God
                    has given to you?
            Oh,
                    yes,
            oh, wait a little while,
            just wait a little while.
            Just wait a little while.

Don't lose faith
      and don't give up courage.
Oh, wait on the Lord.
Oh, wait on the Lord,
Oh,
Just wait on him. Just wait on him.
He'll lead you across your Red Seas.
He'll make you overcome your enemies.
He'll bring every Pharaoh down
      to be your footstool
         if you'll just wait a little while.
If you'll just wait a little while—
you may be standing now
      before your Red Seas,
you may be standing now
      before your enemies,
but oh, wait on the Lord.
      Did you hear what I said?
I said, just wait on the Lord.
Oh.
Oh, wait on the Lord.
He'll make sure
      he's with you.
He'll make sure.

9

Ye Must Be Born Again

[*Nicodemus Meets Jesus;
Seeing the Kingdom of God*].
Chess LP-17.
Recorded ca. mid-1950s.

. . . on a passage selected from the book of St. John, the third chapter, beginning with the first and a few of the following verses: "There was a man of the Pharisees, named Nicodemus, a ruler of the Jews: the same came to Jesus by night, and said unto him, Rabbi, we know that thou art a teacher come from God: for no man can do these miracles that thou doth, except God be with him. Jesus answered and said unto him, Verily, verily, I say unto thee, Except a man be born again, he cannot see the kingdom of heaven."

Seeing the kingdom. That's what we're talking about. Seeing the kingdom.

It is thought that Jesus was stopping in the home of one of his disciples when Nicodemus visited him on this epochal night, desirous to interview Jesus on the question of being born again. Being born again. You see, we are concerned about Nicodemus, number one as to who he was. First of all, he was a Pharisee. He was a member of that exclusive sect in Judaism who set themselves apart as being the guardians of the law. You see, the law had two groups of sponsors, the Sadducees, who were the exponents of the written law, the Pharisees, who were the exponents with the oral law, who believed that simultaneous with the giving of the written law, God gave certain gifts to certain people to interpret that law called the oral law. Aside from that, these people considered themselves a distinctive group because they harked back to the Maccabean campaign, which got under way to purify Judaism and to liberate the Jewish people from the desecration of the Assyrians. And these people tied themselves to that noteworthy history with respect and in relation to Judaism. Not only were they the interpreters of the law but they called themselves the guardians of the law, the guardians and the exponents of a purified Judaism.

Now aside from that, Nicodemus was, or enjoyed some distinction aside from his membership in the Pharisaic party. He was a ruler of the Jews, he was a member of the Sanhedrin council, and the Sanhedrin council was a kind of a supreme court in Judaism, a kind of a supreme court. Now it was this type of man, a man who was a Pharisee, a man who was a strict religionist, a court justice so to speak, who came to Jesus by night.

Now there's been some speculation as to why he chose to come by night. Some speculate that he was ashamed. Others felt that possibly his occupation, his profession, his job, his work preoccupied him and rendered him unable to see Jesus during the day and that the nighttime was the only convenient time for him. Be that as it may. But what I think is really important is that he went to Jesus. That's the important thing. No matter about the time. The great thing is that he went to Jesus. Doesn't make any difference about what time it is; day or night's all right. The important thing, the thing that you should not allow or dare to put off, and that is to see Jesus, to see Jesus, see Jesus.

And then upon his visit he addressed him, he exhibited a unique respect for Jesus. This man—ah, I think if there was any real reason for visiting Jesus by night, I think it would be that Jesus had not been sanctioned by Judaism, the leaders, the high priests, the church, the nation had not accepted Jesus, they had not sanctioned Jesus, and this man was a public official and a great deal of importance was attached to him interviewing or visiting with anybody. Isn't it so? And so possibly for public reasons, for reasons that were concerned about his public conduct, possibly influenced him to see Jesus by night.

But despite the reason of his visit or the time of his visit, he had a unique respect for Jesus. Notice his address: "Rabbi." Rabbi. You see, a rabbi was a teacher, he was a teacher of Judaism, he was a preserver of Judaism, he taught in the synagogue, he was one of the guardians of preserving the cultural heritage and the religious heritage of the people of Judaism. He was an important man. And remember that these people didn't play, didn't just play around with titles. If he addressed Jesus as rabbi it was because he respected him as such. For a Jew did not address you or associate you with that which he regarded as sacred and religious unless he was so impressed by you. (I wish I had somebody here praying with me tonight while I'm trying to preach sick here. Listen if you please. Listen if you please. Listen if you please.)

So he addressed Jesus as a rabbi, and then he indicated that Jesus had been the subject of discussion and the subject of consideration not only by him but by his associates. Listen at him: "*We* know—." It's more than me been thinking about this thing. *We* know. "We have not only thought, we have concluded. We know that thou art a teacher sent from God." (I wish you'd pray with me.) "We know that thou art a teacher sent from God for you couldn't do these miracles that you were doing except God was with you. But sir, I'm a little puzzled. I was in one of your audiences on a previous occasion, and your subject, your teaching, your preaching embraced a strange subject, the subject of being born again. Now I'm not an illiterate man. I'm a man who's versed in jurisprudence. I'm conversant with current philosophies. I know what the Greeks think and I know what the ancient thinking of the Babylonians was, and I know what the Romans think. I'm kind of up-to-date on current matters, but this philosophy that you are talking about, this being born again kind of gets me. Scientifically I can't figure that out. From the standpoint of genetics I can't see it." (Pray with me if you please.) "What about this being born again? Do you mean to say that I've got to disintegrate, go back into nothing, and then come forth again through the same process?"

Jesus said, "Now, your thinking is materialistic. The thing that I'm talking about is a spiritual thing. It has to do with the will, it has to do with the heart, it has to do with the soul. It doesn't have to do with the body. It influences the body. Yes, it influences the body's choice, the body's ability to choose; it influences the disposition of the body, but it's a spiritual thing. And aside from that, don't marvel over it, you *must* be born again. It's imperative, it's mandatory. That is, if you expect to see, comprehend, and understand the kingdom, you've got to be born again." (I wish you'd pray with me.)

You see we have a lot of folk in the church who are not of the church. We have a lot of folk whose names are here but whose souls are not here. We have a lot of folk who cannot see or appreciate or understand what the church is doing? You know why? Jesus said you couldn't see it if you hadn't been born into it. (I wish you'd pray with me.)

I want to say to you, any world, in order to see it, you must be born into it. Let us take for example the physical world. You can't stand on the outside of this planet and see and appreciate and understand what's going on on it. If you would appreciate the pale splendor of yonder's moon, if you would appreciate the unique beauty of yonder's star, if you would respond to the blushing beauty of yonder's rose, if you would behold the quiet majesty of yonder's mountain, you must be born into this world. Otherwise you can't see it, you can't see it. You cannot see physical things unless you've had a physical birth.

And that's not only true in the world of physics, it's true in the social world. You cannot appreciate the order of society, no society, unless you've been born and integrated into that society. Isn't it so? A little boy walks into the grocerman's store, holding on to his father's hand. He looks on the counter and sees there in fanciful paper beautiful cakes. He sees there fruit to challenge and tease his appetite. And he walks up to the counter and gets all the cakes that he wants without even looking at the grocer or feeling any sense of responsibility to him. You know why? That little boy has not been born socially. He has not been integrated into the social order. He has not learned the laws of what is mine is mine and what is thine is thine. No no, he sees the cakes and he knows that he wants them and that's all that really matters to him. Isn't it so? But when he has experienced a social birth and has been integrated and comprehends the total social picture as to its demands and obligations, if he wants the cakes he goes into his pocket and pulls out the price. But he can't see all of that or none of that until he has been born socially. (I wish I had somebody here that was praying with me.)

Isn't it so? Listen if you please. Listen if you please. It is said that once in Italy there was a great crowd visiting one of the world-famed art galleries. (I'm going to bring this home pretty soon.) And that crowd was milling through quietly and standing before the great creations of the great immortals as if they were praying, as if they were awestricken. Another woman who had no appreciation for art and for extraordinary creations in paint looked in and saw all of this crowd of folk and said to the custodian, "What are all these folk doing here?" The custodian said, "Well, madam, this is a world-famed art gallery." She looked up on the wall with unseeing eyes and said, "I don't see nothing but pictures." You see, to her they were pictures and only pictures because she had not been born into that world. She had no appreciation, no understanding, no sense of comprehension because she had not been born into that world. She could not see its beauty, she could not see its value, she couldn't see anything about it in a comprehensive way, because as Jesus said, before you can do that you must be born into that world.

My brothers and my sisters, I don't worry too much about people who criticize the church and who say that there is nothing to it and that there is nothing to the Christians. You don't need but a little sense to even appreciate the church. When you think about the great import and the great impact of the Christian idea on world society, when you think about what this world would be like if Jesus and his followers had never been on this planet, you could appreciate the church. I don't worry too much about it, I don't bother too much about it, because those folk have not been born into this world. And if you have not been born into it you cannot see it. The singing doesn't mean anything to you. The preaching doesn't mean anything to you. The efforts and the work, the great job that the church has done through the ages, mean nothing to you because you can't see it. And if you haven't been born into it you can't see it.

You know I believe that most of you were born in the South and know something about a tadpole. You've heard of a tadpole, haven't you? A tadpole, you understand, is one of those little water creatures that looks like a catfish. He resembles a catfish to a large degree. And he is capable, however, of being something else. He is usually found around stale and stagnant waters.

And he contents himself in that stale, stagnant, muddy water, you know, for quite some time. And then Mother Nature whispers to him and tells him that he doesn't have to be satisfied with merely being a tadpole. Mother Nature tells him that he's able and capable of being something else.   [Whooping:]

> But before he can be that something else
> why, he must go through a process
>> that's called metamorphosis.

And
> that catfish
> or that tadpole
>> must go down
>> in the muck and mire
> and go down there
>> and stay there.

And
> while he's waiting down there a process sets in
> and that process starts
>> to working on
>> that old tadpole.
> And while that process is working,

why,
> that tadpole
>> is changing.

And
> when the process is over,

why,
> that old tadpole
>> has turned into a frog.
> He can leap out
>> of that muddy water.

And
> he can leap out
>> of that stale water.

Oh, yes.
> He can come on out
>> of those stagnant waters
> and leap up on the bank
> and jump around
>> in the grass

and
> jump around

among the flowers
and
      set on a log late at night
and
      in his own peculiar style
           sing praises
           to his God.
O Lord.
Why,
      but he never could have enjoyed
           any of this
           if he hadn't gone
           through a change.
O Lord.
      And I don't know
           about you, my friend.
      Not Mother Nature,
no, no
      but the God of Nature
      whispered to me one day
      as Mother Nature did
           to the tadpole
           and said,
      "If you're a sinner
           in your sins
      you don't have to be satisfied
           with what you are.
      You can be an heir of God
           and a joint heir with Jesus Christ.
O Lord.
      You can have a home
           on high.
      You can be an inheritor
           of the things in the sky.
      But before you can do this
           you've got to go down,
      go down
           on bended knees,
      go down
           in humility,
      go down
           in

an effort to seek God's
        pardon for your sins.
O Lord.
    If you'll stay there
    a spiritual metamorphosis
        will set in your soul.
Oh, yes it will.
O Lord.
    And when
        the process is over,
o Lord,
    when the change
        has been finished,
o Lord,
    you may have been
        a sinner,
    but you arise
        a new creature.
Yes you will.
    Oh yes.
    You'll arise
        and walk in the newness
        of life."
        Yes.
    Yes.
    Maybe you don't know what I'm talking about.
    Oh yes.
    Somebody said
        when it was all over,
    "I stood up on my feet,
        yes I did,
    and looked at my hands,
    and yes my hands
        looked brand-new.
        Yes they did."
    Somebody
    said, "Looked like the clothes
        that I had on
        looked brand-new."
    Yes.
    Yes.
    Yes.

Yes.
If you know what I'm talking about.
Yes.
You know you are a new creature.
   Yes Lord.
Somebody said
that "Not only did my hands
   look brand-new,
but all
[?]
Oh.
   Yes.
Yes,
   looked like a new creature.
Yes,
   yes I raised my hands,
   yes and cried.
Born again.
You must be,
   you must be,
you must be born
   if you'd understand.

10

Give Me This Mountain

[*Asking God for Big Things*].
Chess LP-27.
Recorded late 1950s.

"Now therefore, give me this mountain . . ." [Joshua 14:12]
Asking God for big things. Asking God for big things.

There was an old minister in Mississippi who used to pastor out near a little rural community or any rural community near a small village town by the name of Tutwiler. The minister is now asleep. He passed on a few years ago. He used to say on Sunday nights in his services, "Children, we're going to have a big time tonight. We're going to aim at the moon but if we fall among the stars we will still be on high ground." And so I think there is a great deal of philosophy, there is a great deal of logic, there is a great deal of truth, there's wholesome advice, not only in connection with worship services or any kind of services as for that matter. I think throughout the whole of our lives we ought to aim at the moon, and if we fall among the stars we'll still be on high ground.

Some people are too easily satisfied. Some people have never arisen to their better or best selves. All of us cannot be the best, but we certainly all can be our best. And very seldom do we have incentive enough to rise to the best that's in us. We compromise, we stop at "That will do." We do not strive and aim high and then work to achieve that aim. Many of you who are listening to me tonight could be so much further in life, could be so much stronger in grace, if you really tried. Some of you could be better church members, some of you could be better husbands, some of you could be better providers, but for the fact that you have become satisfied with what you are and what you're doing.

Some of you complain about what you do not have. Don't you know if you really tried you could have that very thing that you're complaining about? Your aim is not high enough, and if it is high you do not work hard enough to achieve it. You ought to do like Caleb did in the text: turn your eyes away from the ease of life, lift your gaze toward the mountain range of possibilities, lift your eyes toward the mountain range of accomplishments, and pick out one of the topmost peaks and say, "Lord, give me this mountain. Give me. I know it will cost me a little something. I know I must suffer and sacrifice. But Lord, give it to me." And if you'll back up that prayer with faith, with determination, with courage, with perseverance, God will give it to you. (I wished I had somebody here to pray with me tonight.)

You know, Caleb had been with the Israelitic armed forces for quite some time. He had been there as a strong young soldier when Israel went through the Exodus from Egypt. He was there when they were complaining at the Red Sea. He was there when they were doubting the ability of Moses' leadership. He was there when the armies of Pharaoh marched on them and God wrought a miracle in the Red Sea. When the people started grumbling and wanted to go back to the fleshpots of Egypt he was right there. He was there when they marched through the wilderness of Paran and the valley of Kadesh. He was there when Israel started to grumbling and wanted to start an insurrection and put Moses to death, when God came down and took Sinai for his pulpit and electrified the mountain with his presence and Israel heard his voice like thunder and closed their ears trembling, saying "Moses, tell him to hush; we'll hear you!" He was right there.

He was right there when Moses launched a campaign to investigate the promised land, to learn its strongholds, to learn its military installations, to learn the odds that he'd have to go up against. He was there and he was among those who were commissioned to go on this mission of espionage. Of the twelve that were sent only two came back with an optimistic report. Ten of the twelve who went over there came back with a report saying, "We can't do it. We can't do it; the cities are too strong. We can't do it; the men are too large, too tall, too giantlike. We can't do it. We can't do it; the city is too securely and the country too securely defended. We can't do it." Only two who said, "We can. Oh yes, we saw the walled cities. Oh yes, we saw the fortresses of the country, we saw the tall, giantlike men. But we can do it." The ten said, "We are like grasshoppers before those strong tall men." Well now, you know life is like that. If you think you are a grasshopper, you are a grasshopper. You are what and can be what you believe you can be. You must have faith first in God and secondly in yourself. That isn't all: you've got to have faith in other people. You, if you doubt God and then doubt yourself and then doubt everybody else you are already defeated. No matter how bad people are you've got to keep on believing that there are some good people around. Oh, I know they can disappoint you. I know they can be real mean sometimes. But you've got to keep on believing in God, in yourself, and in people. (I wished you would pray with me tonight.)

But Caleb, the speaker of this text, was among those who went over to investigate the land but he was not among those who considered themselves grasshoppers in the face of the enemy. He was among those who believed despite the obstacles, despite all of those things that they had to encounter, that they could do the job. And I say to you tonight, if you believe before the onslaught of life that you are a grasshopper, that you are a weakling, and that you cannot do this and you cannot do that, you can't do it. And there are other things in your life that you ought to look around and take stock of yourself and say that "I can do better than this." You know what they are; I don't have to name them. You know the things, you know the shortcomings in your life and in your experiences. You ought to look around yourself and then raise your eyes and your faith above where you are and say, "The Lord will make a way."

This day when the text was uttered Joshua was presiding over a conference at Gilgal. The battles had been fought. The Jebusites and the Moabites and the Amorites had been overrun by the might of Israel. And now that the invasion so far had been successful, they met at Gilgal to divide the land. You know, the people that hadn't been in the foxholes, they were in Gilgal that day. Oh, the crowd is not there when the fighting is hard and severe; the crowd is not there when you're in the trenches. They're not there when the foxholes must be gone into, they're not there when the spadework is being done. But when the day of handouts comes, the crowd is there. Oh, there were representatives of every tribe. And all Israel was there, politicking and plotting and entering into intrigue, trying to get this grant and that grant, seeking the best land, the rolling hills, the meadows, the delta flat and fertile land. They were there that day.

But apart from all of this politicking, and apart from all of the goings-on in Gilgal, there was one strong man, a tall soldier, about eighty-five years of age. Looked back upon a successful and faithful life, a man who knew the horrors of war, a man who knew what it meant to go into the foxholes, a man who knew what it meant to bear the brunt of the load.   [Whooping:]

He stood there that day
    and said to Joshua,
"Why,
    I'm not here" (in so many words)
      "seeking any handouts.
No, no.
    I'm not here
      politicking
      with anybody.
And

I'm not here
in any interest group,
no, no,
trying to get
the best grants.
No, no,
I know I've been in the thick of the battle
all along the way.
I was there
when we went across
the Red Sea,
and
in all of the wilderness
I was there
when the going was rough.
I was right there.
And
I know I've fought well
but I'm not asking for any handout."
"But wait a minute, Caleb.
You're eighty-five years old now
and you ought to,
you ought to be ready
to take a grant and go on off
and retire.
Don't you know
that time
has plowed wrinkles in your face.
And
your body is strong and vigorous
but it won't be long
before the burden of many years
will bow that strong body down.
And don't you know
the mountain that you are asking for
is fenced in,
and don't you know the walls
are strong
and hard to surmount?"
"But I'm not worried about that.
Give me
this mountain.

I know I'll have to leave Gilgal
    and go back to the fights.
Yes I will.
    I know I'll have to struggle
        all the way up the hill,
        but give me this mountain.
O Lord.
    Give it to me.
    You know the Lord
        and Moses spoke of me,
        and of my service.
Yes he did.
    And I'm not asking for an easy life.
        Give me the mountain.
    No matter about the sacrifice:
        give me the mountain.
    No matter about the suffering:
        give me the mountain."
    And let me close when I tell you this story.
    They tell me,
Lord God,
    that there was a young man
        who lived in a valley
        near a mountain.
    He'd grown up with
        other boys
        in that mountain community,
and
    these were famous mountains
    and people from all over the world
        came to climb them.
    And this little, weak little boy
        stood there
        looking at its lofty summit,
    and dreaming one day
        that he might climb the mountain.
    And yet he was so weak,
    and yet he was so unambitious
    that nobody thought of him
        as ever climbing it.
O Lord.
    Strong boys

talked about it
> but he kept it to himself.

Yes he did.
> He never thought
>> of telling anybody about his dreams,
>> but he kept on dreaming
>> and he kept on believing.

My God.
> As he grew up he saw men
>> try the mountain.

Yes.
> He saw them start
>> and then fail,
>> and turn around and come back.
> He saw them fall
>> into accidents

and
> he saw many
>> fall to their death.

My God.
> But one day after growing up
>> into manhood,
>> he said, "I'm going to try it.
> I'm going
>> and get me a rope
>> and get me a carpenter.
> I'm going
>> and get me a pup tent
>> and all of my equipment,
> and at the morrow
>> I'm going to start.
> If I fail
>> I'm going to start anyhow.
> If I fall down
>> I'm going to start.
> If I fall even to my death
>> I'm going to try.

Yes I am."
O Lord.
> And the next morning early
>> he got started,
> climbing on up

the mountain,
going a little higher
and a little higher.
And watching the evening sun
as the sun went down.
Great God.
And
in the evening
when the shadows'd fall
he'd stretch his tent,
o Lord,
and lay there
until early in the morning.
And then early in the morning
he'd climb a little higher.
Yes.
And all day long
he'd be going around
and going up,
going around
and going a little higher.
O Lord.
Slipping back sometime,
but going on anyhow.
Losing his foothold,
but going on anyhow.
Yes.
O Lord.
And then one day
he reached yonder summit
and stood on the roof of the world,
my God,
with the flag of his country
in his hand,
and
planted it
in the name of the country.

Yes.
I'm going to close when I tell you this.
I'm climbing
life's mountain.

Yes I am.
    I'm going
        round by round.
Yes.
    Every day,
        every day.
    Every day
        I'm getting a little higher
        and then a little higher.
    Every day,
    every day,
        I'm making another round.
    Every day,
        yes.
    They're laughing at me sometimes.
    I'm falling back sometimes,
        but I'm getting up going on
        a little higher and a little higher.
    O Lord.
    Yes!
    Yes.
    Oh one of these days.
    Ohh!
    Ohh! one of these days.
    One of these old days.
    I'll make it
    to yonder's height,
        yes I will.
    One of these days
        climbing will be over.
    One of these days
        struggling will be over.
    One of these old days.
    Ohh!
    Oh.
    Ohh! one of these days.
    Ohh! one of these days.
    Ohh! one of these days.
    Yes.
    Yes.
    One of these days.
    I wonder do you know what I'm talking about?

Are you climbing,
        are you climbing tonight?
Ohh!
O Lord.
Ohh!
Ohh! one of these days.
Ohh! one of these days.
One of these old days.
One of these days
        I will.
Are you climbing now?
Are you [?]
Or are you going on anyhow?
Ohh!
O Lord.
Lord one of these days.
Lord one of these days.
Oh yes!
Yes.
The race will be over
        one of these days.

Barbara and C. L. Franklin, ca. 1950. Photographer unknown. Courtesy of Rachel Franklin.

C. L. Franklin with his children. L-R: Cecil, Erma, C. L. Franklin, Carolyn, Aretha. Detroit, ca. early 1950s. Photographer unknown. Courtesy of Erma Franklin.

C. L. Franklin with Joe Von Battle in his recording studio. Franklin's albums were released on the JVB label before they were leased to Chess. Detroit, ca. mid-1950s. Photo by Edward McLaughlin. Courtesy of Erma Franklin.

C. L. Franklin (L), Prophet Jones (in white fur coat), others unknown. Detroit, April 10, 1953. Photo by K. D. Modernistic Photo Studio. Courtesy of Erma Franklin.

Clara Ward, ca. mid-1950s. Photographer unknown. Courtesy of Erma Franklin.

C. L. Franklin preaching, ca. late 1950s. Photographer unknown. Courtesy of Erma Franklin.

C. L. Franklin outside his Detroit home, ca. late 1950s. Photographer unknown. Courtesy of Erma Franklin.

C. L. Franklin, Ambassador Edith Sampson, and Senator Ted Kennedy. Taken at Jimmy Carter's inauguration, Washington, D.C., January 20, 1977. Photographer unknown. Courtesy of Erma Franklin.

L-R: Benjamin McFall, Martin Luther King, Jr., C. L. Franklin. Detroit, ca. 1963. Photo by Edwards Photo. Courtesy of Erma Franklin.

C. L. Franklin with Coretta Scott King. Taken at New Bethel Baptist Church, June 24, 1963. Mrs. King was their Women's Day speaker. Photographer unknown. Courtesy of Erma Franklin.

New Bethel Baptist Church, the new building, ca. mid-1960s. Franklin is standing to the right of the pulpit desk. Photographer unknown. Courtesy of Erma Franklin.

C. L. Franklin preaching, New Bethel Baptist Church, October 30, 1977. Photo by Jeff Titon.

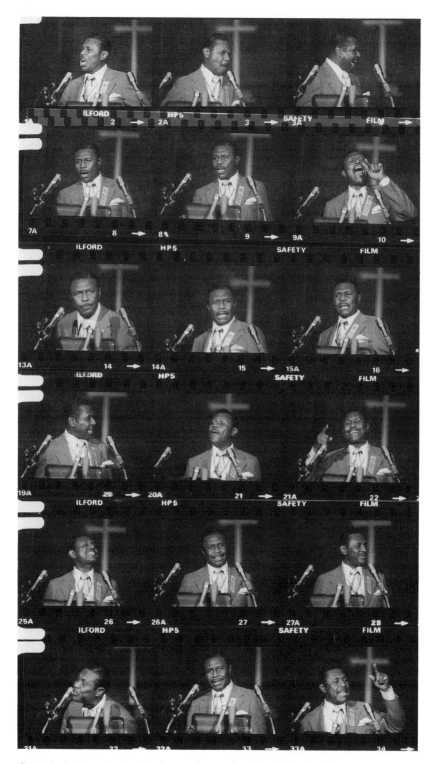

Contact sheet of C. L. Franklin preaching, New Bethel Baptist Church, May 28, 1978. Photo by Jeff Titon.

C. L. Franklin preaching, New Bethel Baptist Church, May 28, 1978. Photo by Jeff Titon.

11

The Man
at the Pool

[*Jesus at Bethesda*].
Chess LP-26.
Recorded in the late 1950s.

[Franklin probably began by quoting John 5:1–9.] Jesus at Bethesda.

The passage that we have selected tonight presents to our mind and to our consideration the case of a man who had been the victim of a dreadful malady for quite a number of years. The exact time is not known. The record only reveals that he had been around this pool thirty-eight years. How long he had suffered previously we do not know. We do know that there was a feast going on in Jerusalem and Jesus was in attendance. For you see, Jesus was a strict observer of the religious traditions of his people. He kept the Sabbath, but he did not allow the Sabbath to restrain him from helping somebody. He observed the feast, but he kept an eye out even at the feast for those who were in need, so that he was loyal to the traditions of his people.

And on this occasion, he arrived in Jerusalem. And if you had chosen, or if it had been possible for you to have been in Jerusalem, and some situation arose that necessitated your seeking out the whereabouts of Jesus with a town full of people engaged in feasting, where would you have looked? Would you have sought out the merrymakers? Not only where would you look for Jesus, where would you have been? Would you have been with the crowd of merrymakers? Would you have been with the crowd that was engaged in festivities and parties? In that case you would have missed Jesus, for Jesus went down to Bethesda. Bethesda—the very word means house of mercy, where an aggregation of people who were ill, a collection of broken, shattered human beings—people who could not join the fast crowds, people who could not take any part in any amount of revelry or merrymaking, people who were confined to one of the five porches at Bethesda.

And Jesus went there. And upon his arrival he sought out the worst case, the most chronic case, the hardest case at Bethesda. He arrived at

Bethesda and walked along the aisles of the five porches looking with compassion on this feverish brow and upon that feverish brow, and possibly stroking the brow of another on another porch, saying an encouraging word here and there. But destiny had set a date with Jesus, or set a date for Jesus with this man who had been there thirty-eight years. And he did not stop walking the porches until he had found him.

Now upon his approach to this man's bed, looking down on his broken and fevered and dwindling body, the first question was, "Do you want to be made whole?" Think about that. What a challenging question, what an engaging question, what a searching question. "Do you want to be?" He did not ask him, or he did not say to him, "Do you want me to make you whole?" No no, no no. He did not say, "Would you like to get away from here?" No no, but "Do you want to be made whole?" Made whole.

You see wholeness is completion, perfection. (Pray with me if you please.) Wholeness is the existence of normality. Wholeness is when things are as they should be. So that one may be physically whole but lacking in wholeness in mentality. One may be mentally whole and spiritually lame. (I wished I had somebody here to pray with me tonight.) It so happened, however, that consideration was for this man physically as well as spiritually. "Do you want to be made whole?"

And you know this is one of the most important questions, one of the most important decisions to be made with respect to everybody. Not only with respect to this man at Bethesda but somewhere along the line you must face this question: "Do you want to be?" Mother, it's a good thing, it's wonderful for you to be ambitious for your son, it's wonderful for you to have great dreams for him, and to plan a great future for him. But the great question is, does he want to be what you want him to be? You may fret yourself and run yourself into all kinds of neuroses trying to do something for somebody that don't want it themself. You see, this is a thing that has to do with a will. This is a thing that has to do with individual initiative. Wife, you'd do well to wipe your eyes and quit crying and quit talking all night, trying to tell that husband what you think that he ought to do for the betterment of the family. The great question is, does he want a good family? Husband, it's high time that you stopped thinking about that wayward wife who has no concern about saving for the future, about forethought for the future, who spent all of her time in the night-houses, and in nightlife, and you're worrying and talking. The great question is whether *she* is concerned. Does she want to be a good wife? Does she want to be a homemaker? That's the great question. Some folk you have so much trouble with because you have not considered whether *they* want to be. And you may want it ever so bad, but if they are not interested it doesn't mean too much.

"Do you want to be?" Jesus knew the importance of this question.

He knew the challenge. To think about this at first may seem that that was an unnecessary question to be asked of a man who'd been down there thirty-eight years, a man who had been to the pool and had been disappointed thirty-eight years, a man who had struggled and crawled to get near the water only to see somebody step in just before he made it. Might have seemed like a funny question to ask that man, "Do you want to be made whole?" But Jesus knew he'd never get up off that bed if he didn't want to first. Those of you who are listening to me tonight on your sickbeds, some of your trouble must be taken care of by you. Yes, the doctor can do a lot. His medication will help, his skill at surgery will help, but then medicine doesn't do it all. And surgery is not the complete job. Some of this must be done by you. Along with surgery, along with medication, must go your desire to get well. (I wished I had somebody here to pray with me tonight.) Oh, this may not be true in every case but if you really want to, if you really get it down in your heart, down in your will, down in your disposition, somehow with a little prayer and a lot of faith, somehow God will bring you out. (Listen if you please.)

This man had been disappointed thirty-eight times. Thirty-eight times he'd possibly resigned and had possibly given up. Thirty-eight times he possibly lapsed into negligence and indifference, and just simply resigned to just staying here as long as God would permit him, and going on when he couldn't do anything else. I feel that too many people in hospitals tonight, too many people in sanitariums tonight, have resigned. You've got to keep in mind the words of Jesus: "Do you want to be made whole?"

You know sometimes we get a real desire mixed up with imagination. There are a lot of things that we imagine we want that we really don't really want. Isn't it so? We really haven't really decided. We imagine and we think about it but we have not really gotten down to real desire or prayer. You know prayer is a little more than just bowing down saying some words. Prayer is first of all, first of all faith in God, and believing, my brothers and sisters, that God is. And believing secondly that you are his child. And believing thirdly that he's interested in you. (I wished I had somebody here to pray with me.)

This man, I said, had been disappointed. He, I don't know, he evidently was not an attractive patient. He evidently was one of those patients that people shunned. It might have been his condition, might have been his condition. But the thing that struck me when I read the story was that I [whooping:]

> wondered why in all
> > that thirty-eight years
> somebody had not
> > given him a hand.
> Wonder why in all of that thirty-eight years

somebody had not aided him
          to the pool.
It was thought of traditionally
          by these people
that once a year that angel came down
          and troubled the waters.
And
          when that water
                    was troubled,
why,
          divine perfection
                    was left in the water,
and
          whoever
          got to the water in time
                    would be made whole.
          But I want to tell you
                    tonight,
          Jesus
          is still
                    at Bethesda.
          Jesus is still
                    at the house of mercy
and
          the water
                    is still being troubled.
          For you see
          the Lord
          still has
                    his Bethesdas around.
          And he still has
          his healing waters
                    around.
O Lord.
And
          in fact
          he has
          a better
                    Bethesda
          today than
                    possibly in that day.
And

at least better than that one
   was at Jerusalem.

For

  in Jerusalem only one man
    could be made whole.

O Lord.

  (I do believe you're praying with me.
  I feel pretty good tonight.)
  In Jerusalem only one man could be made whole.
  And if the other one didn't get in first,
  he had to go back,
  as the man in the story,
  and lay down on his bed
    for another year.

O Lord.

  But I want to tell you
  the Lord
  still has his Bethesdas
    in Detroit.
  He has them not only in Detroit,
    he has them in America.
  And not only in America,
  his Bethesdas are all over the world.

Yes.

  And he has hosts
    and legions of angels,
  every day
    and then every hour
    troubling the water.

Yes he has.
Lord.

  And the only thing you have to do
  is step in by faith
  and he'll do the job for you.
    Yes he will.

O Lord.

  Every day
  an angel is coming down
    troubling the water.
  If you have a malady
  of selfishness,
  you ought to step in tonight.

If you have a malady
of bad-heartedness,
you ought to step in tonight.
Lord, Lord.
If you have a bad heart,
you ought to step in tonight.
Yes.

If you have an evil mind,
you ought to step in tonight
and let my Lord make you whole.
Yes.

And even if you're on a sickbed,
and even if you're in a sanitarium,
you can step in tonight.
Yes.

Every day,
          every day,
every day,
          and then every hour,
my Lord is at the pool.
Lord, Lord.
Every day,
          yes,
oh yes.
You ought to see him today,
when you pass the pool today.
Every,
every hour,
ah yes,
my Lord
is waiting right now
for you to step in.
Ohh.

One Thursday morning,
one Thursday morning,
one Thursday morning,
in 1929
I stepped in for myself,
yes I did.
Early!
Early,
early!

Early!
Early!
Early!
Early!
My Lord!
[?]
let me step in.

12

Except I Shall See in His Hands the Print of the Nails and Thrust My Hand into His Side

[*Doubting Thomas*].
Battle 6102. Reissued as Chess LP-54.
Recorded ca. late 1950s.

We call your attention to the book of St. John, the twentieth chapter, the twenty-fourth through the twenty-ninth verses. "But Thomas, one of the twelve, called Didymus, was not with them when Jesus came. The other disciples therefore said unto him, We have seen the Lord. But he said unto them, Except I shall see in his hands the print of the nails, and put my finger into the print of the nails, and thrust my hand into his side, I will not believe. And after eight days again his disciples were within, and Thomas with them. Then came Jesus, the doors being shut, and stood in the midst, and said, Peace be unto you. Then said he to Thomas, Reach hither thy hand and thrust it into my side, and be not faithless, but believing. And Thomas answered and said unto him, My Lord and my God. Jesus saith unto him, Thomas, because thou hast seen me, thou hast believed. Blessed are they that have not seen and yet believeth."

Doubting Thomas. Doubting Thomas.

The passage that I have read in your hearing tonight deals with one of the post-Resurrection incidents. If you can call upon your knowledge of history, and upon your powers of imagination, you could picture the hostile world in which these followers of Jesus found themselves. The Jewish hierarchy had put their leader to death. He had been tried and condemned by the Jewish church, by the Roman courts, and he had been nailed to a tree while they looked on. They had seen him drop his head after a terrible experience during the night of trial, scourging, and crucifixion, that ended on Friday evening about three o'clock. They heard him say after that terrible night, "It is finished." You know how they must have felt when they had chosen to follow him, when they had accepted him as their Messiah, the anointed of God.

And now the man whom they had called the Son of God, was now dead, and apparently disgraced. And of course you know how they must have felt. Some of them said, "Well, I'm going back to fishing. I'm going back to my old job. I'm going back to my old vocation. It seems that we made a mistake." I believe Peter made the suggestion, and the others followed his lead.

Thomas, who was of the scientific turn of mind, heard some rumors. The women had said that they had seen him, and that he was alive. Others said that they were en route to Emmaus, and he joined them and talked with them and while he talked their hearts burned. Some of the rest of them reported that they had seen him. Lately it was said that in their secret gathering place in Jerusalem to avoid the police and to avoid arrest and embarrassment, that he had come into their meetings.

But Thomas said, "I don't believe it. I don't believe it. Obviously you're being swept by rumors or you're suffering from hallucinations. Nobody has ever died as I saw that man die, and come back again. I was looking at them when they hung him to the tree. I was looking at them when they nailed his hands and his feet. I was looking when the soldier thrust the sword into his side. And I heard him when he dropped his head say, 'It is finished.' And I saw them take him down from the cross and lay him in Joseph's tomb. I know he's dead. Now there's only one way that you can ever tell me anything different, and that is I'll have to see him. And I'm not going to trust that. He is going to have to show me his hands, and let me see the nail prints in his hands. He will have to let me look at his side, and then I will have to examine his side for myself. I must satisfy the sense of seeing and of feeling before I shall be convinced. I don't believe that he's alive."

Now Thomas, called Didymus, which means the twin, has received a great deal of ridicule from the Christian world about his doubting position. But you know, you must give some respect to people who want to know, to people who are not satisfied with hearsay. You must give some respect to people who want to base their faith upon as much knowledge as they can acquire. You see, superstition, rumor and hearsay is not a sufficient foundation for faith. I know that faith transcends knowledge, but you get all the knowledge you can get before you stop. For you see, Thomas was moving on fact. And you see fact can carry you just so far. It was a fact that Jesus was put to death, that he was hanged to a tree. It was a fact that he dropped his head and died, and declared, "It is finished." This was a fact. It was a fact that they took him down and laid him in a tomb. All of this was fact. But that is as far as fact could go. This is the reason that Thomas couldn't go any further: because he was proceeding on the basis of fact. You understand what I'm talking about. His whole operation was based upon empiricism, investigation and what one can find out. But you see, faith—you understand what I mean—goes on beyond the grave. (I don't believe you know what I'm talking about.)

Faith doesn't stop at the grave. Faith didn't stop when he said, "It is finished." Faith didn't stop when they rolled the stone to the tomb. And faith didn't stop when the governor's seal was placed thereon. For you see faith goes beyond what I can see and what I know. I can't prove God. And you don't have to prove God. Somebody said, "If you haven't seen God or you haven't seen heaven," and all that kind of thing—. That doesn't mean anything. Say, "Who's been there?" That doesn't mean anything, what you cannot prove. What you cannot see is no argument against its existence. You can't see electricity but God knows it exists. You can't see energy, but take all the energy out of this room tonight and all of us would be dead shortly. Hmm? Many of the forces of the universe, you can't prove them, you can't see them, you can't touch them, but they do exist. They are realities. (I don't believe you know what I'm talking about.)

But Thomas was like many of you that are listening at me tonight. He wanted to base his faith totally upon fact. Totally upon faith, or rather upon fact. But you see faith moves out beyond what I can touch, beyond what I can see, beyond sometimes what I can hear, and even beyond what I can investigate. I don't know where God is, but I believe he liveth. I don't know anything about how he raised his Son. I'm not concerned about whether it was bodily or spiritual. I believe that Jesus liveth tonight. I believe that he is a living reality. He is a transforming influence in this old world of ours. Don't you know all of these people wouldn't have been following him by the thousands and by the millions for twenty centuries if he didn't live? Don't you know all of these people who go to their graves with his name on their lips, saying, "Death cannot make my soul afraid if God be with me there, though I walk through the darkest shades, I'll never yield to fear," if he didn't live tonight? (I don't believe you know what I'm talking about.) The great impact that his name has had upon history would not have changed the world society if he wasn't a living influence. I believe he liveth.

So Thomas wasn't at the meetings. And you know when you fail to meet constantly with that Christian fellowship, you miss so much. You miss so much in inspiration, you miss so much in God-consciousness, you miss so much in soul-enrichment, when you fail to fellowship with that Christian society. (I don't believe you know what I'm talking about.) So Thomas's great mistake was he wasn't there. And when he came in after having given voice to his doubts, he eventually presented himself at one of the services. And while they were no doubt musing and meditating upon God, singing his praises, while they were no doubt talking about the fact of his Resurrection, while they were no doubt talking about their faith in the fact that he was alive—, without

a door being opened he walked in. And thank God he can walk in here
without a door being opened. He can walk in to your life sometime when you
unconsciously open the door. The door of your life might be open and you
don't know it. He can walk in. While they were in their meeting he walked
in, without a door or window being opened.   [Whooping:]

And
       when they looked around
           he was standing in their midst.
When
       they looked around
           he was there
           in their presence.
       And it seemed that,
why,
       his address
           was so consoling.
       He knew how
           doubtful some of them were.
And
       he knew how afraid
           some of them had been.
And
       he knew how their faith
           had been tried.
And
       he knew what a terrible ordeal
           they'd gone through.
       And think about how
       consoling
           his address was.
       Listen at him: "Peace be unto you."
O Lord.
       You know when I think about
           the world that we live in,
       when I think about
           how frustrated
           many of us are,
       when I think about how
           neurotic we've become,
       when I think about
           how tension-filled

many of our lives are,
when I think about
how afraid of life
so many of us are,
why,
I think about what Jesus said,
to those fearing
and doubting disciples.
"Peace be unto you."
Great God.
You that are afraid tonight,
great day,
you that are anxious tonight,
and
you that don't know how
to face your problems,
you ought to hear his word
coming down through the centuries,
saying "Peace be unto you."
O Lord.
Though the storms
may rage around you,
though the road
that you are traveling
may be rough,
though the problem that you're faced with
may be perplexing,
o Lord,
he'll still say to you,
"Peace be unto you."
O Lord.
"Peace be unto you."
O Lord.
Listen.
Did you know what Thomas said
when
he beheld the reality
of Jesus Christ?
You know what Thomas said
when he saw
his wounded hands,
when he beheld

        his wounded side?
"My Lord,
        and my God."
Great God.
     And I'm going to close when I tell you this.
O Lord.
     I'm not going to wait
        until I behold
        the wounds in his hands.
O Lord.
     I'm not going to wait
        until I behold the wounds
        in his feet.
     I'm not going to wait
        until I have a chance
        to behold the wounds in his side.
     I'm going
        to acknowledge him as Lord
        right now,
         every day of my life.
O Lord.
     Would you be my guide,
     would you be my real leader,
     would you lead me through the crises of life?
     I've got to stop right here.
O Lord.
     Yes,
     the winds that blow me about,
     yes,
     my faith is tried sometime,
     but I'm going to hold on
        to his unchanging hand.
Yes I am.
     Yes every day,
     every day,
     yes every day,
     every day of my life,
     I'm going to hold on,
     in the midst of doubting,
     in the midst of the windstorm,
     in the midst of failure,
     in the midst of frustration,

I'm going to hold on anyhow.
Oh.
O Lord.
Oh yes.
Yes.
For he is my Lord,
and he is my God.

[Speaking:] He is the Lord of my life. He is the Lord of my life.
He reigns and he liveth. He liveth. [Singing:]

Maybe you don't believe it,
        but God is real tonight.
        God is real tonight.
Sometimes Satan
        tries to
        make me doubt.
He tells me
        that there are a lot of things that I imagine
        are not so.
He tries to tell me that I'm caught up
        in the grip of
        my traditional upbringing;
        that God is not real.
But if God is not real
who is it
that watch over me every night?
Oh
        who is it
        that calms the storms about me
        if he's not real?
Tell me who is it?
Who is it
that makes me cry
when there ain't nobody hurting me,
that makes a fire burn
        down in my soul?
Who is it?
If it's not the Lord,
        then who is it
        that makes me run sometimes
        when nobody's behind me?
God is real.

13

Hannah,
The Ideal Mother

Chess LP-65.
Originally issued, with portions missing, on Battle 6112.
Recorded ca. late 1950s.

"And when the time was that Elkanah offered to give to Peninnah his wife, and to all her sons and her daughters, portions: But unto Hannah he gave a worthy portion; for he loved Hannah: but the Lord had shut up her womb. And her adversary also provoked her sore, for to make her fret, because the Lord had shut up her womb. And as he did so year by year, when she went up to the house of the Lord, so she provoked her; therefore she wept, and did not eat. Then said Elkanah her husband to her, Hannah, why weepeth thou? and why eateth thou not? and why is thy heart grieved? am I not better to thee than ten sons? So Hannah rose up after they had eaten in Shiloh, and after they had drunk. Now Eli the priest sat upon a seat by a post of the temple of the Lord. And she was in bitterness of soul, and prayed unto the Lord, and wept sore. And she vowed a vow, and said, 'O Lord of hosts, if thou wilt indeed look on the affliction of thy handmaid, and remember me, and not forget thine handmaid, but will give unto thine handmaid a man child, then I will give him unto the Lord all the days of his life, and there shall no razor come upon his head.' " [I Samuel 1:4–11]

Hannah, the ideal mother.

I've simply read this for your consideration, and that we might, while we think on Mother's Day and its significance, and what it means that in these days when people are detouring from the path of the traditional pattern of motherhood, then possibly our thinking and our talking will influence us to reconsider our ways. A great deal of sentiment has been built around this day. A great many tributes are made to mothers. Since this day has been set apart by Congress as Mother's Day, of course people are communicating and expressing their respects and their love and their appreciations for mothers in any number of different ways—by telegrams, by letters, by cards, by gifts, and by any number of ways to say, "I appreciate my mother. I love and I respect my mother."

Yesterday I was in one of the cleaning places getting a shoeshine on John R [Street] and a young lady began talking to me about Mother's Day and told me that her mother had passed on. And she said, "I wish she was here. I would do thus and so for her tomorrow." But among the many things I want you to remember on this Mother's Day is, let us not only have special Mother's Days. Let us let every day be Mother's Day.

And to the young modern mothers, to the twentieth-century mothers, to the atomic-age mothers, let us remember that if you would have the eternal respect of your descendants, you must be deserving. For today all mothers, I think, are not acting like mothers. You know there are those who say that they do not believe in divorce. Be that as it may, it seems to me that that assumption is based on the idea that "Let that which God has joined together, let no man put it asunder." But you can't tell me, I don't believe that all the folk that are married today, God joined them together! As I have said before, people marry for too many different reasons, and some of those reasons are not good ones. And so I think that some people would be better off if they did not have children. At least I know the children would be better off! (Are you praying with me?) I think that a mother should follow a certain course of action, should possess a certain attitude toward her children. In the first place, a real mother should have some sense of what the idea of motherhood really means. It means a little more than to merely bear children. It means a little more than that.

In the first place, the person who brings children into the world is highly honored. You are performing thereby a divine duty and responsibility. And no matter what your attitude may be about it, with the bringing forth of children come responsibilities and obligations. Whether you like it or not, God has so endowed you and has enabled you to bring forth children into the world, and you become the steward, the God-appointed guardian over those children. You cannot always determine what they will do, but what you can do, you can do the best you know how to imbue into them certain ideas that will be guideposts and warnings and stops in their lives.

Oh, to our dismay and to our utter regret, we are often grieved at the course that our children take. They take courses that we had hoped they would avoid, but even with that possibility, and even with that prospect, we are responsible to do the best we know how: what God expects us to do for our sons and our daughters.

And there seems to be something close, a little bit closer than father, about mother. For you see, mothers usually teach their children the first words that they utter. No wonder they call it, the language that we speak, our mother tongue, because usually we learn it from mother. The mother who believes in God not only teaches her children the first utterances, the first audible and intelligible words that they speak, but she teaches them the first things that they know about God. That is, if she knows anything about God. So that I think, and I would to God that it were left to me, I think that every mother ought to be a Christian. I don't think that a mother is really equipped, is really prepared, to bring up children if she herself does not know God. I think that mothers figure too definitely in the ideas, in the outlooks, and in the attitudes, and in the dispositions that her children possess to not first know God. And since she figures in the ideas, in the disposition, in the views, in the outlook, in the attitudes of her children, and since that person must grow up to mingle and associate and work with other folk, I think the person who coaches them, those children in their plastic years, in their years what they call the impressionistic years, that person ought to know God.

Pardon me for being personal and using myself as an example, but I'm saying this because it happened in my own experience. I learned how to pray from my mother. I never knew what prayer was until I learned it from her. And her faith in God was contagious for me. As I reflect back down the vista of the past today, as I think about all of the problems and all of the experiences that I have had, through all of the years that I have lived, without a faith in God, and without faith in prayer, and without a disposition of loyalty to God, I don't know what I would have done. I don't know what I would have done. Without believing in prayer, without believing in prayer, without faith in God, and ultimately faith in myself, the trials and the tests and all of the responsibilities that I have gone through, I believe, would have shattered me. Had it not been for my faith in God, and my faith in myself, which I inherited from my mother, I don't think I could have taken it. I don't think I could have taken it.

Listen if you please. Hannah, [whom] we have chosen as our model mother today, was one of those mothers who desired to be a mother. You know, we have become so modern today, until it's a little old-fashioned to have children. In the society that Hannah lived [in], it was an honorable thing to have children, and every mother, or every woman looked forward with desire, and with respect toward the state of motherhood. She wanted [to be] a mother. The woman today who has more than one child, or more than two children, is very often the object of criticism, and sometimes downright scorn. Say, "Honey, you know she's having too many children, she's losing her shape."

I'm using these terms to impress it upon your minds that these expressions are indicative of a deeper attitude, and of an attitude toward family life that's undergoing basic changes. You see, there is immortality in your offspring. The immortality of the family, the constancy of the family, was so important in Eastern and Oriental society, that the idea of carrying on the family name and the family tradition was so important that if one brother died without having or bringing forth children to carry on his name, if he had other brothers, the next oldest brother must follow him into wedlock with the wife that he left behind in order that the family name would go on. It was so important.

But today we have changed our attitudes. Hannah, the model mother, had a desire for motherhood, and not only a desire but prayed to God to bless her with the state of motherhood, to bestow upon her motherhood. It was customary that the petitioners, the parishioners of the priests, would take their petitions to the priest and tell him what their desires were. But Hannah deviated from the traditional approach and went up and prayed for herself. She didn't leave it to the priest; she went personally to God for what she wanted. And certainly those of us who live in the Christian era believe in what Hannah did, for we believe in a personal approach to God. (I don't believe you know what I'm talking about.) We believe in going to God for ourselves.

And I think every mother ought to be a praying mother; not only [to] look upon the state of motherhood with respect and view it honorably, but, I think, every mother ought to be a praying mother. It would be a wonderful thing in your home for your children to hear you pray sometime. You don't know the potency, you don't know the extent of the influence that it would have upon your child's life in his formative years, for that child to hear you pray sometimes. I never shall forget that when I was a child that frequently I heard my mother pray, and the thing that impressed me most was that occasionally at night I had been awakened out of my sleep with tears from her eyes dropping in my face, saying, "Lord, help me to rear my children, help me to rear them as God-fearing children." Listen. Listen. To hear her telling God that for me, to hear her say, "Lord help me to rear them," and then, "Help me to rear them as God-fearing children, help me to keep them in a path that will give God glory," went a long ways in my mind and toward influencing my disposition. You ought to let your children hear you talk to God for them sometimes. Hannah was a praying mother. Not only did she have an esteemed respect for the state of motherhood but she was a praying mother. (Pray with me if you please.)

And then thirdly (and I'm going to be just about through when I say this), thirdly, she rededicated her children to God. Can I tell you a bit more that's personal and has to do with my own experience? Of course, the approach would probably be criticized today. But when I was a boy, my mother used to, on Sunday mornings, I didn't have any shoes to wear to Sunday school, [and] she'd have me to grease my legs and walk proudly to the Sunday school. Mmm? And, you know, the Sunday school provided those little cards with pictures on them for the children. And she would take my sister and I over these cards several times. "Read it," she would say. Or she'd read it for us and she'd have us following her, reading it to us. And then after she'd gone over it several times with us, then she'd hand it to us and reach back and get a strap and say, "Now you read it!" You know, that gives you pretty good encouragement to read, doesn't it?

Aside from that I recall another thing. These things live with you. I remember one night in the graduation of the year, I guess from about fifth or sixth grade, my sister and I were on the program to speak. And of course the kids were rather noisy and I was rather afraid to stand up before an audience and speak. And this particular night I stood up to speak but I spoke so low that very few people heard me. When I finished speaking I cast my eyes around at my mother and she looked at me a certain way and I knew that I was in for it. She said, when she got home that night, "When I get through with you, the next time you get up on the stage to speak, you are going to speak." And believe it or not, I've been speaking ever since then! And I mean speaking where folk could hear me.

Now this is not an approach that child psychology would recommend in the upbringing of children, but I want to tell you it certainly was an effective approach so far as I was concerned. And it certainly has done some positive things for me—some positive things, some things that have serviced me and have helped me through my life in the years that I have lived. So I'm trying to say to you, my brothers and my sisters, I think it is necessary that we rethink about the problem of bringing up our children, and that we would reexamine ourselves on shouldering the responsibilities that are imposed upon parents. And, certainly, mother has her place in this scheme of things. For you see, we are largely responsible for our children. We are largely responsible. The Lord gave them to us and the Lord is counting on us to bring them up to live that abundant life and to make the world a better place in which to live. As you look at a baby crying in its mother's arms, as you look at that little span of humanity, the eye, the physical eye cannot analyze the possibilities that's within that child. The physical eye cannot see all the things that he is capable of doing and what he will do and what contribution he will make to world order and to human adjustment, as to what contribution he would make into making the world population a brotherhood.

And [in] making [a] world society, the kingdom of God depends largely on mother as well as on father. My brothers and sisters, this is no small task. This is no small task, and this is no day and age when we should shun the responsibility imposed on us as mothers and fathers. These are your children. And God gave them to you. I never shall forget that before I moved to this city, when I first took over the pastorate of this church, there were three little boys who were left at home one night alone. And I believe, if my memory serves me right, they were left in a room where an old coal stove was, to keep them warm. And about three-thirty or four o'clock in the morning the house caught afire and the little children were suffocating, all three of them, before any help could reach them. And they had to go to the tavern somewhere at that hour in the morning and find that mother and tell her that her children were dead. For you see, this, we could not say, was the ideal mother. (Pray with me if you please.) I believe the little boys were about, let's see, three, four, and five, something around that age, subject to wake up any time of night, subject to need any kind of aid, or any kind of help, subject to wake up sick, and, my brothers and my sisters, and sisters especially, it may be a little sacrificing to stand by the children and to do certain things. It might cause you a lot of trouble. It may put you to a number of inconveniences. But I want to tell you if you'll stand by them, they never will forget you. [Whooping:]

    And they'll rise up in their own time
        and call you blessed.
        Call you blessed.
    Oh, you may say to yourself,
        "Children today don't appreciate
        anything that you do for them."
    You may say that "Children are so wild
        and are so bad
    that they don't appreciate
        the sacrifices
        that I am making for them.
And that
    I'm going to work,
        and working long hours,
    I'm rising early in the morning,
        and they don't realize what I'm doing,
    and that girl
    that I deny myself for
        to let her look all right,
why,
    she doesn't have time
        to do anything.
    Her mind is on folly
        and on pleasure."
    But I want to tell you
    the time will come
        when her mind will change
        and her whole attitude will change.
    The time will come
        when she'll look back on your sacrifices

and

    the time will come
    when she'll look back on the trouble
          that you had

and

    will say,
    "I don't see how
          she stood it all."

And

    "I don't see how
    she was able
          to go through with all the trouble
          that I gave her."

And

    I want to say this other thing to you is

that

    I believe when you reach old age,
          (I wish somebody would pray with me),

and

    when your head
    has begun blooming
          for the grave,

and

    when you reach that age
    when life has purged your mind
          of folly

and

    time
    has settled your
    mind and your attitude
          as well as your body down,

then

    I believe it's a wonderful thing
          to have a son or a daughter
    to say to you, "Mother,
    I still love you,
          for you stood by me,

and

    I appreciate all the things
          that you did for me.
    In my coming up maybe
    I acted like I didn't appreciate it,

but it was only because I didn't understand you then.
But now
I know what you were trying
to do.

And

I want you to remember
the time
that you put in
is not lost."
It may take a little time
for them to see what you are after,

and

it may take a little time
for them to understand what you were trying to do,

but

I know
from my own experience,
and I know from my broad
contacts,
and I know from the thousands
of children that I've talked to in my life,

o Lord,

those who were brought up properly
still hold on to it
and look back on their parents
with reverence and respect.

Holy God.

Occasionally
they may go wild
and they may go astray.
As I remember having heard a story
of a young woman
whose eyes
caught the light of the world.

And

who was bewitched and allured
by the bright lights of the night,

and

looked on her old mother
as fogey and old-timey,
and got with a fast crowd
and turned from her upbringing.

When mother talked to her
and prayed with her
and pleaded with her,
she became so tired
until eventually
she left town,
and said, "I'm going to leave here,
for I can't have any fun
      without mother bothering with me all the time
      and criticizing me all the time."
And that lady,
      that young lady went to a distant city
      and got with the fast crowds,

and

      eventually she lost
         her health

and

      went to the tuberculosis
         asylum.

And

      she lay there
      with her body wasting away
         and her lungs deteriorating.

And,
o Lord,

      as she lay there, her whole life
      like a panorama
         came before her.
      It came to her
      how difficult she'd been,
      and how hard she had been,
      and how prone she was
         to go wrong.

O Lord.

      It came to her
      that mother, after all,
      knew what she was talking about.
      Maybe what she said
      did not spark her
      into wild, ardent living,

o Lord,

      but mother knew

what all of this
　　　　would come to.
O Lord.
Yes.
　　　　She'd been in town several years.
　　　　She had not been so nice as
　　　　to write mother and tell her where she was
　　　　　　　　or give her her address.
　　　　And as she lay there on the bed,
great God,
　　　　she said, "I would like to write her
　　　　　　　　and let her know what has happened to me.
O Lord.
　　　　But I've been so bad,
　　　　and I've gone along so long
　　　　　　　　without dropping her a line,
o Lord,
　　　　I do believe
　　　　I feel ashamed of myself
　　　　to get down on a sickbed
　　　　　　　　and then write her.
　　　　In all the years of my health
　　　　and my youth when I was running around,
　　　　　　　　I didn't have time to write her.
　　　　The crowd was carrying me too fast
　　　　and too many things were going on
　　　　　　　　for me to take time to write to her.
O Lord."
　　　　But the end,
　　　　the end seemed to have been coming.
Great God almighty.
　　　　She said to her friend,
　　　　"It doesn't seem
　　　　　　　　that I'll be here much longer.
　　　　Ohh.
　　　　I know I've been wrong.
　　　　Would you come down
　　　　　　　　to the hospital
　　　　and set down by my bed
　　　　　　　　and write and tell her,
　　　　let me tell her before I go
　　　　　　　　that now I appreciate her

and now I understand.
O Lord.
I don't want to lay down and die
without letting her know
that I learned that she was right.
O Lord."
And when that mother
got the letter
as she read down
along the lines
about the condition of her child,
tears
began to roll down her eyes
and she began thinking in terms
of "How I can get there and get her
and bring her home.
And if the Lord wants to take her,
let him take her
from home."
O Lord.
And
she walked in that hospital
with tears streaming down,
said, "Daughter,
I'm not thinking about what you did.
You're my child.
You were just young
and didn't know any better.
O Lord.
I'm trying to make arrangements
to take you on back home.
I know
that you were a bit wild,
yes I do.
I know,
I know.
I know!
Good Lord.
Yes I know.
Ohh
yes I know
that you were a little fast

and that you were a little headstrong,
but you're still my child.
O Lord.
    I know
            that you didn't have the experience that mother had
            and you didn't know what you were getting into.
        Ohh!
            Come and go home with me
    and I'm going to stick by you.
    Every day and every night I'm going to pray for you."
O Lord.
    And [she] nursed that girl back to health.
            Let me tell you,
            let me tell you,
            it may not be the thing that you want to do
            but you better have ears and hear somebody
            that knows some things that you haven't learned yet.
Isn't it so?
    Thank God
            for mine
    who told me
    that the Lord
            is a door
            when every other door is closed,
    that the Lord,
            yes the Lord,
    ohh the Lord,
    is a way out of no way,
            when there is no way.

[Speaking:] Thank God for learning that, and thank God for learning it early. Thank God that it has stood by me and has borne me over many a flood. Thank God it has been a guiding light in my otherwise dark life. Thank God it has been an arrow of direction when I would have otherwise been confused. God bless you.

14

The Foolish and
the Wise Builders

[*A House Built on Sand*].
Chess LP-38.
Recorded prior to 1963.

In the book of St. Matthew, the seventh chapter, the twenty-fourth and one or two of the following verses, we read as follows: "Therefore, whosoever heareth these sayings of mine, and doeth them, I will liken him unto a wise man which built his house upon a rock: and the rain descended, and the floods came, and the winds blew, and beat upon that house; and it fell not: for it was founded upon a rock. And every one that heareth these sayings of mine, and doeth them not, shall be likened unto a foolish man, which built his house upon the sand: and the rain descended, and the flood came, and the wind blew, and beat upon that house; and it fell, and great was its fall."

The foolish and the wise builders. The foolish and the wise builders.

There has always been something unique about the parables of Jesus. I think that I have made this observation before, and that is that the parables of Jesus are so unique, so graphic, so overwhelming that the centuries cannot wipe them from our minds, or free our thinking of the memory of them. Not that Orientals had not told stories and parables and allegories previous to Jesus. Many of them told them well. You have only to read Judaistic literature previous to the time of Jesus. Read the rabbinical writings, read even in the Old Testament and we will find many parables and allegories and stories. But none of them took on the quality of eternity such as did the stories and parables of Jesus. Who can forget the Prodigal Son? Who can forget the story of the Good Samaritan? Who can forget the story of the man who sold all that he had to buy something else that he had discovered that was more valuable? Who can forget the story of the Five Wise Virgins and the Five Foolish Virgins? These stories will live as long as time lives.

And so tonight we are concerned and we invite your meditation on the story of the Wise and Foolish Builders. In this connection Jesus is dealing with the business of living, the business of living. He's talking about building lives substantial enough to withstand the storms of life. And I think in times like these, when there is so much fear, when there is so much anxiety, when our insane asylums are so crowded and feeblemindedness is so rampant, when people are so neurotic—we would do well to think about the business of living, of living contented, adjusted lives, living God-centered lives, living lives that are God-influenced. (I wished I had someone here that would pray with me while I'm talking about this.)

Oh, we're advanced in many other things. We are way out in front in technology and in the sciences, in the military. We are way out in front when it comes to production and all that kind of things. When it comes to the building of homes and improving communities from the sanitary standpoint, we are pretty advanced along those fronts. But we are a little behind in the business of living. Oh, we are ultramodern in our automobiles and in our modern homes. Why, we are way out in front when it comes to our new types of planes, our jet planes and what have you. But I'm afraid that we are living a couple of centuries behind when it comes to man's adjustment with man. (I wish you'd pray with me tonight; you must don't know what I'm talking about.)

For we don't burn pine knots and coal-oil lamps any more. We don't live in houses that the ceilings are too high too much anymore, because we realize it's a waste of fuel, it's too hard to heat them. We don't ride in the old T-model Fords any more. We think in terms of futuramic automobiles. But I'm afraid that when it comes to human relations we're a little antique. We haven't made much improvement upon our social adjustments. We have the same old evils, the same old tricks, the same old savagery, the same old backwardness that we used to have. (I wish you'd pray with me.) There's still inhumanity to man. There's still exploitation of labor. There's still a struggle of the workers to get justice for their labor. There's still lynching and burning. There's still murder and all kinds of injustice. I think we need to turn our minds to the business of building lives and finding human adjustments. (I don't believe you're praying with me tonight.)

Jesus said if you're going to build a house of your moral existence, if you're going to build a house in which you're going to dwell morally all your life, you better build it well. (I don't believe you know what I mean.) You better build it well. In telling this story, Jesus carried the note of urgency throughout the story. He not only carried the note of urgency but also in harmony another note comes in, and that is the note of authority. For he that heareth these things and doeth them is like a wise man who builds his house on the rocks. And as Luke said, digs down until he finds the rock. The man that doeth them not is like the foolish man who builds his house on the sands.

You see, my brothers and sisters, we build our lives and our home, our character homes, as a carpenter and as a builder builds a building. You see, when we come to the level of existence where we are impressive and conscious of those impressions, we begin to lay the foundations. Every emotion, every volition, every idea might be a brick on our character home. Thus the foundation ought to be deep, it ought to be deep. The foundation ought to be deep. You see, each time we acquire an attitude, each time we develop a disposition, we reach in and get another brick going in on the building.

And you see, there are important things about a building. Number one is the foundation, the girders and the pillars as to so far as what that house can stand depends upon its foundation. Its pillars and girders, if those are not strong, it can't stand too much of a load. (I don't believe you know what I'm talking about.) This is so important and so essential until the administration sees to it that we build by codes, by regulation and by specifications. And not only are you required to do so, but a man is on salary to check every now and then and see if you are building according to those regulations.

If that is true in building homes, it's certainly true in building lives: the foundation ought to be strong; the girders of every life ought to be strong. (You understand what I'm talking about.) The walls, the pillars, the rafters ought to be strong. These are why so many lives go to pieces: the foundation is bad. Reason why so many lives crumble in, the girders are not strong enough and they couldn't stand the load. No, no, a building that's built for one story, it's folly to try to make three or four stories or put the load of three or four stories on that building. (I wonder are you praying with me tonight.) Isn't it so? We've got to build strong.

And you know, the house that you build, your character home, your moral home, is a home no matter how frail, no matter how little forethought has gone into it, it's a house that you must live in. There's no question about that: you can't change. No sir, you can't lease it and change and get you another house, and you can't sublet it and you can't rent it out. You've got to live in it yourself. Oh, the foundation may be shallow and the walls may be flimsy; the girders may be weak and the pillars may be very frail, but if that is the way that you have built it, that's the house that you've got to live in. And if there's any repair to be done, you've got to do it. You've got to do it. Nobody can do it for you.

You know, in the kind of houses that we build to live in, these human houses, on the outside they all look alike. Seldom unless a person is extremely neurotic, can you look at that moral house of his, except you have known him and know something about his deportment and conduct, you can't tell a good house from a bad one. Outwardly they all look alike. Your house looks like mine. Mine looks like yours. And some weak houses may look better than some strong houses. You can't look on the outside and tell what the house can carry. You can't tell. Some frail-looking houses are very strong houses. When you go inside and go down into the basement and look at the foundation, you'll say, "This house was built well." But some very good-looking houses will crumble in the first wind, so that you can't tell from outward appearance. It takes the windstorms of life to test the kind of house that you build for shelter in life. Oh yes, let the thunder growl and rumble in the distance. Let life's thunder, that's what I'm talking about, let life's thunder start growling. Let life's lightning start tearing the skies of life. Let the torrential rains of life pour down. (I wish you'd pray with me.) Let the floods of life fill the riverbeds of life and flow out into where your house is and then we'll know whether your house can stand. Then we'll know. Circumstances do not always make too much difference. Circumstances certainly are important but sometimes the best houses are built in bad circumstances and sometimes some of the worst houses are built in better circumstances. So it takes life to test what kind of house you're building.

I have seen men in my lifetime in great teams, various groups of subcontractors, go to a building and take their machinery along with them. I've seen them go to the trouble of digging up the earth. It seemed like to me that the earth was solid. It looked like to a layman's eyes that it was just as well to build right there, on top of the ground. To my untrained eyes it seemed like too much trouble and too much expense were being entered into in the attempt to build the building that they had undertaken. But these men knew about buildings.   [Whooping:]

> These men had been trained
> > about building buildings.
> And these men had taken in
> > the account of the cost
> of how high
> > the building was,
> and how heavy
> > the load that the building
> > would have to carry.

And

> they knew
> according
> > to their training,

and

> according
> > to the builder's code,
> it's necessary
> > to dig down a little bit.
> Not just a short ways,

         but go way down
until the kind
       of solid earth
       had been discovered,
and
       start there,
          pouring
          the forms of the
          concrete footing.
O Lord.
       (I don't believe you're praying with me tonight.)
And
       you ought to see these men
          building up the walls,
yes,
       making them strong,
yes,
and
       shoring them
          as they went along,
       pouring the floor,
          solid,
       making the walls
          substantial,
       including
       steel
          in the walls sometimes
       so that
if a
       rock set in
       and the concrete failed,
       the steel
          would insure.
Yes,
o Lord.
       It's a lot of trouble,
       but they built on
          just that way.
Yes.
       It takes a long time,
yes,
       but the men know

that if there's going to be
    a substantial building,
    you'll have to put a little time in it.
O Lord.
    So the life
        that would be a successful life,
    that life ought to be
        built well,
    it ought to dig down
        into life.
O Lord.
    Before
        it gets to its foundation
    every life
        ought to dig down,
    and if you'll dig down deep enough
        you'll find a rock
        even in life.
O Lord.
    For Jesus,
    is the rock of our lives,
o Lord.
    If you'll dig down
    far enough
        you'll find him.
    And when you find him,
        you ought to start building
        right from there.
    You ought to pour
    the footing of faith,
yes,
    so that
    when you've made your foundation,
        you've got a strong footing.
O Lord.
    You ought to put the steel
    of prayer and hope
    throughout the wall,
yes,
    so that when faith can't see
        you can hope on anyhow.
    (I don't know if you know what I'm talking about.)

O Lord.
      Yes.
      The walls ought to be strong.
Yes.
      The walls
      of good will,
      the walls
      of neighborliness,
      the walls
      of kindness,
      the walls
      of mercy
      and of truth and honesty
            ought to be in your building.
O Lord.
      If you'll build of those walls
            everything will be all right.
      If truth is there,
      if faith is there,
      if love is one of your walls,
and
      if honesty is there,
o Lord,
      the winds may turn a-loose against you,
            but stay there anyhow.
O Lord.
      (I don't believe you know what I'm talking about tonight.)
Yes.
      You ought to cover the old building
            with prayer,
yes you ought to.
      You ought to have
      the windows of the soul
            in your building,
      so that the soul
      may look out on life sometimes,
      and help you make your decisions
            sometimes.
Lord God almighty.
O Lord.
      I remember
            having heard a story

as I come to my conclusion.
The story is
that up in Lebanon
there are
        cedars on the mountainsides,
yes,
    and they tell me those cedars
        grow down.
    They are not so tall,
but
    they're strong
        and dependable.
    Those roots go down
        into the mountain.
    Go down
        until they strike a rock,
    and then those roots fanwise
        around the rock
    and go on under beneath the rock,
    and wrap and tie themselves
        under the rock,
o Lord,
    so that when the winds
    and the storms let loose,
    those old cedars just rock
        from side to side.
Yes.
    And when the storm is over
        they stand up again,
        strong.
    You ought to build like that,
o Lord,
    let the roots of your faith
    go down in the mountain of salvation
    until it strike the rock
    of salvation,
o Lord.
    And as you go on through this old world,
        and experiences in life
    begin to rock you from side to side,
        stand there.
    Yes!

        Let the wind blow.
Yes!
Yes.
Yes!
Let life rock you
        from side to side,
        but stay there anyhow.
Yes!
Yes, yes.
Stay right there.
Stay right there.
Ohh!
Be sure that you're strong.

And

        be sure
                that you dug deep
                and sounded well.

O Lord.

        Yes!
Yes, yes.
Stand there.
Stay right there
                until everything's all right.
Stay there
until you are sure
                the foundation is all right.

15

What of the Night?

[*Watchman, What of the Night?*].
Chess LP-75.
Recorded between 1956 and 1963.

"The burden of Dumah. He calleth to me out of Seir, Watchman, what of the night? Watchman, what of the night? The watchman said, The morning cometh, and also the night: if ye will enquire, enquire ye: return, come." [Isaiah 21:11–12]

The subject: Watchman, What of the Night?

This passage, according to all authoritative commentaries, is a prophecy of the doom of Edom. It is a prophecy of the aggression and the ultimate triumph of the military forces of Persia over Edom. This military victory that brought on for Edom oppression, placed Edom in such a dilemma that Edom cried out in her confusion and frustration, having experienced this transition, "Watchman, what of the night? Watchman, will our plight be better or worse now that we are under a new government, now that we are in the orbit of a new political power? What will our lot be?"

Watchmen, in the scheme of Oriental things, were important people. They watched cities; they watched communities; they stood upon lofty walls; and the security of these cities and these communities depended upon the alertness of these watchmen: for while the city slept, these watchmen watched. They watched for invading armies; they watched for what you would call raids on the part of raiding bands; and they gave the city, or the respective community, notice of the approaching enemy. So that the figure here, on the part of either Isaiah or that anonymous writer that is given the credit of having written that part of the book of Isaiah after the exile—either Isaiah or the anonymous Isaiah—is saying in this chapter, that because of the plight of Edom, which is referred to here in terms of Dumah, the burden of Dumah, for Dumah was a place in Edom, and this Hebraic prophet declared that in a vision, the dilemma of Edom reached him as he stood upon the lofty wall of vision, and in vision he heard the cry of frustration, and the cry of oppression, coming out of Dumah, and out of Edom, and that cry was an inquiring cry: "Watchman, what of the night? What of the times? What time of history is this? What time of trouble is this?" For after all, history is God's big clock. For a day is but a thousand years in terms of eternity. (I wish somebody here would pray with me.)

History is but—or a day is but a thousand years [i.e., a thousand years is but a day]—so that history is God's big clock; and inasmuch as we cannot see within the next five minutes, in our system of time—in God's system of time, in God's clock of history, we can't see—we must call out to our men of vision, we must call out to our prophets, as Edom or as the Edomites did in those long days, or bygone days: [to] men who can pierce the future; men who can interpret the future; men who can see beyond now; and inquire of them, "Watchman, what of the night? What time is this? What time of history is this? What hour in God's purpose and in God's plan is this? Like the Edomites, what will our lot be?" The future is uncertain to us, and we must make anxious inquiries, for we don't know. We are blinded by the night, we are blinded by the mystery of history, we are blinded by the density of time. (I wish you'd pray with me.)

For to us, it is like it was with John; for John said, he saw an angel standing with a scroll rolled in his hand, and it was sealed on all sides, and nobody could break the seals or read the writing therein, but the lambs. So we know that history is God's scroll, already sealed, written within and without; and we cannot read the writing, and we cannot break the seal; only God can reveal it to us, or reveal it to his men of mystery. And so, as the Edomites did, thousands of years ago, with the anxiety of the future, with questions of the future, we inquire to the men of vision, who walk upon the lofty walls of God's inspiration, "Watchman, what of the night?" (I don't believe you know what I'm talking about.)

For, after all, my brothers and sisters, we are living in times that are like the nighttimes. We don't know what the morning will bring. We don't know. We know that Africa is rumbling, that Africa is awakening like a sleeping giant, and that on the horizon we see the Gold Coast emerging as an independent nation. We see the Sudan that has come into independence as a young nation. We see Egypt, having seized and nationalized the Suez Canal. We have seen the English and the French and the Israelite forces, military forces that is, rush across her borders, and then be stopped by the mild force of the United Nations in order to pull out and go back to their own lands. We see Hungaria [Hungary] on the march, defying the pressure and the desire of international Communism to subjugate her. We have witnessed over a hundred thousand of Hungarian citizens fleeing across the Hungarian borders, into Austria. We see tension in Germany between East and West Germany. We see Poland resisting those who would deny her sovereign independence. (I wish somebody would pray with me.) We have heard say that no more is the Big Four America, England, France, and Russia, but rather, America, Russia, India, and China. (I wish you'd pray with me a little while.)

We see these signs, watchman, on the horizon of time. We've seen changes take place in China. We see India, the second great manpower pool in the world, come to a position of international neutrality. (I wish somebody would pray with me.) We see oppressed people, not only abroad, but in our own lands, becoming impatient, for full citizenship. Not only Africa, not only Egypt, not only the Arab world, not only Germany, not only China, not only India, but we see Montgomery, Alabama, we see Florida, we see other parts of our own land impatient for world brotherhood and full citizenship.

We don't know all what these signs mean. We see them, but we are too blind to properly interpret them. And so we call out to our prophets, to our preachers. We call out to our educators, to our philosophers, to our statesmen. We call them watchmen, and we inquire of them, as we view these conflicting signs, "Watchmen, what of the night? What of these times?" (I don't believe you're praying with me.) "What time is it? And what shall we expect, as history unfolds in this new year?" (I wonder are you praying with me?) "What shall we expect?"

The writer here gives us a picture of Oriental travelers who had traveled the deserts in the cool of the evening, and as the night had fallen, they came to the foot of a mountain range. And as they came to that mountain range, they decided to camp rather than to risk traveling in the mountains, rather than to risk the treachery and the dangers of the mountains. They decided to camp in the shadow of that mountain for that night, and wait until the morning comes. The night was long, the night was anxious, the night was trying as they waited to resume their journey the next morning. As they camped, the night was dark. They looked on the mountain ranges. They could see the cedars that crowned the top of the mountain like gory monsters in the dark. They could see the jagged edges of the mountain cliffs; they could hear the water running from mountain springs that made a menacing noise late in the night. (Pray with me if you please.)

The campers became anxious and restless during the night, for indeed, the night was dark, and indeed, the night was trying. And they called out to their watchman, hour after hour, "Watchman, what of the night?" And no doubt when they had checked the time, they went again, feeling that the time had come, and it was time to arise, and it was time for the sun to be up, and time for daylight to break upon men so that they could see their way in resuming their journey. [Whooping:]

And
        as they went to the watchman
and
        thought about it was time
        for the morning light to come,
why,
        they noticed that
        though
        the morning light was breaking,
great God,
and
        though the darkness
                was dispelling,
that
        a new blinding,
        a new blindingness
                was settling over them.
        Did you hear them say,
        "Watchman,
                what of the night?"
"Why,
        the morning comes
                and so does the night."
        What a confusing statement is this.
Why,
        what does it mean
        by "the morning cometh
                and so does the night"?
        Does he mean to say that
        night
                follows the morning?
        for, studying his language,
        that seems to be what he's saying.
        But we know morning
                is not followed by the night.
        Morning
                is followed by the noon,
                and then by the afternoon,
                and then by the evening,
o Lord.
        But the
        inquirer,

great God,
why,
        realizes
        that though the darkness of the night
                has flown away,
        he's blinded
        by new
                darkness.
        And what darkness
                is this?
Well,
        what he is saying,
        and what he's alluding to,
                is this:
well,
        when the sun rose
great God,
        and spreaded
        its warm rays
                in the valleys,
                where the travelers were,
        the cool morning air
        mixed with the warmth of the morning sun,
and
        this conflict
        in atmospheric conditions
                created a fog.
O Lord.
        And the fog
        was more blinding
                than the night.
O Lord.
        For in the night
        they could see
                the top of the mountain.
        In the night
        they could see the jagged edges
                of the mountain ranges.
(I wish somebody knew what I was talking about tonight.)
O Lord.
        In the night
        they could see

the outlines
of the cedars that stood
        on the mountaintop.
But when the morning came,
great God,
        and when the sun rose,
        and the heat
        mingled with the cool air of the morning,
                and created the fog,
o Lord,
        the fog hid the mountain,
        the fog hid the mountain clefts,
        the fog hid
                the cedars
                that stood on the mountain.
O Lord.
        So,
        though the morning has come,
        other confusion has arisen
        that's even worse than the night.
O Lord.
        As we look out
                on history today,
and
        as we look out
                on world situations,
        the night of slavery
                has passed.
Great God.
And
        the night
        of many other oppressing things
                has passed,
        but other
        foggy conditions
                are arising,
yes,
        and we want to inquire,
                of those that can see,
yes,
        we want to inquire
                of those who are standing

in the lofty places,

o Lord,

those that God
would lift on higher ground,
"Watchman,
what of the night?"

O Lord.

"Oh, watchman!
It's mighty dark.

And

how long
will the darkness last?
How long
will we go through this night?
How long
will we blunder through this fog?

O Lord.

Ohh!
When will the skies clear?

O Lord.

Watchman!
We've waited a long time.
Watchman!
We've been restless a long time.
Watchman!"

(I don't believe you know what I'm talking about tonight.)

Yes.
"We've waited a long time.
Ohh!
How long,
how long,
how long,
watchman!
will we be oppressed?
And will we be cast down?

And

watchman!
Would you tell us?
and give us a little light?

And

watchman!
will you give us new hope?

And

    ohh!

          o Lord,

    oh yes,

    we've sung,

    we have prayed,

    we have waited,

    and we have watched;

    tell us how long.

O Lord.

    Watchman!

    Our fathers waited,

    our grandfathers waited,

    and their fathers waited,

    the slaves waited,

    tell us how long!

    Ohh!

          how long,

          just how long?

And

    we have shed tears,

          yes we have,

    we've sung

          "Pharaoh's army got drownded,"

    we've sung

          "Steal away to Jesus,"

    we've sung

          "Swing low, sweet chariot,"

    we've sung

          "We're going to eat at the feasting table,

          one of these old days."

    Ohh! how long,

          just how long?

    Ohh!

          good Lord,

          how long?

O Lord.

    Ohh, a few more days.

    (Did you hear me?) [Singing:]

    A few more days.

    A little while to wait,

    and a little while to pray,

a little while to labor,
a little while to sing.
We're blundering in the dark,
we're toiling in the light,
o, tell us, watchman,
oh, we're waiting on an answer,
oh, how long,
        how long?

16

This Is
My Beloved Son

[*A Mountaintop Vision*].
Chess LP-77.
Recorded prior to 1964.

I call your attention to the book of St. Luke, the ninth chapter, and the thirty-fifth verse: "And there came a voice out of the cloud, saying, This is my beloved Son: hear him." This is my beloved Son: hear him.

I don't think that we have been called upon to do a more important thing than this verse calls upon us tonight to do. And what gives it weight, is, number one, who calls upon us to do it; and, number two, to whom we are called upon to hear. "This is my beloved Son: hear him."

This incident took place, it is thought by authorities, in the community of Caesarea Philippi, in one of the neighboring mountain ranges. The experience itself was called a theophany, an overshadowing of the spell of God. Jesus had ascended into the mountain to pray, as was often his custom to do. Though he was the son of God, and though he had an awareness of God beyond any man who has ever lived and who has ever walked upon this planet, his godliness himself, and his ever-awareness of God, did not make him feel that he did not stand in the need of prayer. He constantly sought the conversation, the presence, and the pleasure of his father. And hence, he secluded himself, he took a retreat, to a mountain.

He took with him on this retreat, three of his so-called favorite disciples, Peter, John, and James. For some reason or other—it might have been natural weariness; it might have been the extensive length of Jesus' prayer, for Jesus did not pray on any schedule. You know, we limit our prayers. All of us, a whole church of us sometimes, only have one hour of prayer. But Jesus did not place any limits on his prayers. If he felt like praying all night, he prayed all night. If he thought that it took forty days, he continued in prayer. One of the sad and tragic things that has happened to the church today [is that] the church doesn't pray anymore. Church people don't pray much [any] more. You don't have big prayer meetings any more. We used to get a crowd of people out to pray, but today if you have a successful prayer meeting, you've got to put something else in it. The church would do well to return to the practice of prayer.

And so, Jesus had these men with him, and like us, they dozed off into a deep sleep. So that these men went off into a deep sleep, but Jesus was preoccupied with something that was heavy upon his heart. Jesus was struggling with something that he knew was inescapable, that he knew was inevitable. He knew that the tragedy of Calvary was unavoidable, and that the pathway that he had chosen, that day in the wilderness, ultimately led to the cross. And so he prayed and mused and meditated and talked with God about it.

In this spiritual atmosphere, in this being caught up in his prayer, in his continuous prayer, during this spiritual theophany, he had heavenly visitors. (I wish somebody would pray with me here tonight.) The disciples forsook him, as it were. They did not leave him physically, but they did leave him from the standpoint of interest. They went to sleep; they left him alone. As they did in Gethsemane, they left him alone. As they did in Gethsemane, they went to sleep.

But while struggling alone, heaven was witnessing the weight of his struggle. (I wish you knew what I was talking about.) An angel saw that his closest friends had gone to sleep. His very closest friends had gone to sleep, and heaven dispatched two visitors to the mountain while he prayed. These visitors were noted visitors, well-known visitors, visitors who left their imprints and their impacts and imports upon time and history. These visitors were Moses and Elias, or Moses and Elijah. That's what we mean when we say Elias. Moses, the exponent of the law; and Elijah, the exponent of prophecy: these two honored and venerated visitors visited with Jesus on the mount of transfiguration while he struggled.

Well, he turned from prayer a little while, and went into conversation with these heavenly travelers. They talked on a theme, and the theme that they talked on, according to the record, was the theme of his decease. Their conversation revolved around Calvary and his death on the cross at Jerusalem. That's what they talked about: they talked about the tragedy of Calvary. They talked about the awfulness of Calvary. They talked about the grossness of sin that could bring the Son of God to the ignominious death on the cross. They talked about the Son of God who was being treated like the son of man. They talked about the holy one who was to be hung up for all sinners. (I wish somebody would pray with me tonight.) They talked about the prince of peace who was to be treated as a prince of devils. That's what they talked about.

And when they had dealt with this great theme and were about to depart, the sleeping disciples woke up. And the theophany was too great; the glory of the occasion was too dazzling, and the experience was too radiant. There was something about it that excited, apparently, other senses of recognition in these disciples. They had never seen Moses before. They had never seen Elijah before. For these folk had been dead hundreds of years before they were born; and yet, when they looked at them, they recognized who they were. (Pray with me if you please.) They recognized who they were.

And I heard Peter exclaim, as the record is, not knowing what he was saying, just being overshadowed, and being overcome, "Master, Lord, we ought to build three tabernacles: one for Moses, one for Elijah, and one for thee. We ought to memorialize this occasion. We ought to set up stones, temples, and landmarks, that the ages would know what happened on these grounds." (I wish you'd pray with me.)

Now when God blotted out Moses, and blotted out Elijah, it was not that the world should ignore them, or ignore their contribution to the world; no, no, it wasn't that. For you see, the law played its part, and prophecy played its part, and Jesus constantly quoted and referred to both law and prophecy. In fact, Jesus could not be understood without the Old Testament. The New Testament would be unintelligible without the Old. (I wish you'd pray with me.) Many of the ceremonies, many of the rites, many of the doctrines, many of the concepts, many of the ideas, would make no sense if we could not find their background in the Old Testament. We would know nothing about the Messiah. We wouldn't know anything about immortality, the kingdom of God and all these things. We wouldn't know anything about what we call "ethical religion" if we did not have the Old Testament to consult. For the Old Testament contains both law and prophecy.

But you see, all of them were just schoolmasters to bring us to Christ. (I don't believe you know what I mean tonight.) They were just schoolmasters to bring us to Christ. Moses did his part in his Thou shalt nots. Moses did his parts in establishing the one God idea, in establishing monotheism. Moses did his part in contributing to the world, ethics and laws, laws that have lived from his time to our very own. His contribution is great today in the world of jurisprudence. No lawyer can ever forget Moses. No law-abiding citizen can ever forget Moses. Moses was on the mountain.

Elijah, when it comes to the ethics of Israelitic religion, he was among those men who taught Israel that God is not so concerned about your pigeons and your doves. What you ought to do is to do justly, love mercy, and walk humbly before your God. A man like that was on the mountain with Jesus.

So, my brothers and sisters, when Peter, John, and James woke up and saw a company of this stature visiting with Jesus in this awful hour, there on the mountain, he exclaimed, "Let us build three tabernacles. Let's leave some landmarks here. Let's leave something here for posterity. Let's leave something here that those who come in generations after us will know what happened on this mountain." But when they were about to be carried away and perpetuate Judaism, when they were about to be carried away and perpetuate possibly a prophecy, as it stood and as it was in that day, a cloud of the Lord overshadowed these heavenly visitors, cut them off from view, and out of that cloud they heard a voice. And that voice was, "This is my beloved Son: hear him." [Whooping:]

Why,
>>you've already heard
>>>>Moses;
>>you've already heard
>>>>Elijah;
>>you've heard
>>>>Jeremiah,
>>>>Ezekiel and Daniel;
>>>>you've heard all of them.
>>You've heard
>>>>what the law had to say,
>>and you've heard
>>>>what prophets had to say.
O Lord.
>>But both law
>>>>and prophecy
>>have been working
>>>>in one direction,
>>>>and that direction
>>>>was toward Jesus.
>>For all that went on
>>>>before Jesus
>>>>was merely working
>>>>up to him.
And
>>so my Lord became
>>the fulfillment
>>of law
>>and prophecy.
O Lord.
>>And so I heard,
>>>>as the cloud rolled past,
and
>>shadowed them out
>>>>and blotted them out,

and
        the voice
                came through the clouds,
        saying, "This is my son.
O Lord.
Why,
        Moses was my son,
                yes.
        Ezekiel was my son,
        Daniel
                was my son,
        Elijah,
                he was my son,
        Amos
and
        Obadiah
                and Zephaniah,
why,
        Jonah
        and all other prophets,
                they were my sons,
o Lord,
but
        this is
                my beloved son,
o Lord,
                and I want you to hear him.
Oh yes.
                I want you to hear him."
O Lord.
        And I'm worried tonight,
        and I'm uneasy tonight,
        and my soul
                is troubled tonight,
for
        I'm afraid,
great God,
        that we [go] around
                building too many tabernacles,
                and not hearing Jesus.
O Lord.
        We're building tabernacles,

great God,
      anywhere
      and for anything
            that overshadows us.
      Anything
            that overwhelms us,
      we're ready
            to make a fetish of it.
      We're ready
            to put it on divine power.
O Lord.
      Some folk
      are making
            tabernacles for politics.
(I don't believe you know what I'm talking about.)
      Some people
      are building tabernacles
            to fraternities.
O Lord.
      Some people
      are building tabernacles
            to pleasure,
isn't it so?
      Some people
      are building tabernacles
      and shrines
            to beauty.
O Lord.
      Some folk
      are building temples,
holy God,
      to youth.
(I don't believe you know what I'm talking about.)
We don't want to grow old.
O Lord.
      We're ready to build a shrine
            to anything.
O Lord.
      Some folk
            are building tabernacles
            to Communism,
            and other wild philosophies.

Isn't it so?
      Some folk
            are willing to build one
            for Prophet Jones,
      and some folk
            are willing to build one
            for Father Divine,
      and some folk
            are willing to build one
            for Daddy Grace,
o Lord,
      but my Lord
            is [?]
            and covering them up
            with a cloud,
      and telling the whole world,
            This is my Son,
            this is my Son,
      this is my beloved Son;
      you ought to hear him.
O Lord.
      And as I close tonight,
            let me tell you,
            you ought to hear him.
      You ought to hear him,
            because he's the Son of God.
(Did you hear what I said?)
      You ought to hear him
            because he has the words of life.
O Lord.
      You ought to hear him
            because history has vindicated him.
Yes,
      and time
            is a witness to him.
      You ought to hear him
            because he has the way
            of eternal life.
      You ought to hear him
            because he's the only one
            that can lead us out [of] our dilemmas
            and guide us out of our darkness.

O Lord.
        You ought to hear him
                because he has a lamp,
                the light in salvation
                in his hands.
        You ought to hear him.
        You ought to hear him
                because he's a way-provider,
                and then he's a way-maker.
Isn't it so?
        You ought to hear him tonight.
        You ought to hear him
        for he has the words
                of eternal life.
        I don't believe you know it tonight;
                you ought to hear him.
        I wonder,
        are you in tune to him?
                listening to him?
        If we'd ever have brotherhood,
well,
        if men in the world would ever get along,
yes,
        if this old war-torn world will ever have peace,
                you'd better hear him,
                you'd better hear him.
        If you'd have peace in your life,
                you'd better hear him.
        "This is my beloved Son:
                hear him."
        Every,
                every nation ought to hear him.
        Every street
                ought to hear him,
        and every community
                ought to hear him.
Yes.
        And every father and mother
                ought to hear him,
        and every deacon
        and every choir member
                ought to hear him,

and every usher,
         and every member,
and every preacher
         and every trustee ought to hear him.
You ought to hear Jesus tonight.
Oh, listen to him.
You ought to listen to him,
you ought to hear him tonight,
saying,
If you're low,
         come on to me.
You that are weary,
you that are out and down,
ohh!
come on to me.
You ought to hear him tonight.
You ought to hear a little prayer.
If you are blundering around in the dark,
Ohh!
         yes,
ohh!
         come on in.

17

The Preacher
Who Got Drunk

Chess LP-71.
Recorded ca. 1969.

We ask you to consider at this time, the book of Genesis, the ninth chapter, the twentieth and a few of the following verses. It reads: "And Noah began to be an husbandman, and he planted a vineyard: And he drank of the wine, and was drunken; and he was uncovered within his tent. And Ham, the father of Canaan, saw the nakedness of his father, and told his two brethren without. And Shem and Japheth took a garment and laid it upon both their shoulders, and went backwards, and covered the nakedness of their father; and their faces were backward, and they saw not their father's nakedness. And Noah awoke from his wine and knew what his younger son had done to him. And he said, Cursed be Canaan; a servant of servants shall he be unto his brethren. And he said, Blessed be the Lord God of Shem; and Canaan shall be his servant. And God shall enlarge Japheth, and he shall dwell in the tents of Shem; and Canaan shall be his servant. And Noah lived after the flood three hundred and fifty years."

The title of our sermon tonight is, The Preacher Who Got Drunk. The Preacher Who Got Drunk.

Now, I thought maybe in using a title like this, that this would at least arouse your curiosity to the point of coming to see who was it, what preacher was it that got drunk, and I might get a chance to tell you some other things you need to know. Thus we ask you now to think with us on this passage.

First of all, we have chosen to talk to you from that part of the Bible which is sometimes called the Pentateuch, or the Books of the Law. It is classified or referred to, sometimes, as the creation[?]. That is to say that it is a Hebraic, poetic story of creation. (Did you get me? If you're following what I'm saying and you're scared to say amen, just bow your head or something so I'm sure you understand me.) I said the reason it is called the creation, this means that it is an historic, Hebraic interpretation of the creation of the world.

Many of the lay people in the church, and a great many of the preachers, so far as that goes—many of the laymen, and a great many of the preachers, do not know that this is not the only interpretation or story of how the world began. (Wake up my deacon there so he can hear me.) It's not the only story of how the world came into being. The Egyptians had a creation story; the Babylonians had a creation story; the Chinese and the Indians, the East Indians to be specific—most of the older cultures had stories of creation.

You know, when I was a boy going to Sunday school, there wasn't too much knowledge about theology. The smartest man in the class was the man who could ask the hardest questions. However, this is not always indicative of smartness. Sometimes people who know less can ask you the hardest questions. So, as a boy, I frequently used to hear the question, When Cain killed Abel, and went into the land of Nod, and found his wife and knew her, where was the land of Nod, and were there any other people there? Whatever or wherever Nod was, I'm here to tell you tonight, there were people there, because the Hebrews were not the only people in the world. So the writer of this story in Genesis is giving a Hebrew version of how the world began. And this is not to say that they were the only people in the world. God has always had other people. (I don't believe you hear me tonight.) There were some Chinese around, there were some Japanese around, there were some Indians around, and some other people. So it's not too strange to conceive that when Cain ran away as a fugitive from justice, that he found other people, just as you would find other people if you went into another land. They did not have modern communications such as we have, but although they were primitive they did exist.

Now these stories, when we study how we got our Bible, including the Noah story that we are concerned about tonight, these stories came down to us by oral transmission; that is, these stories were told around the campfires for centuries, and as they were told by word of mouth for centuries, for generations upon generations until the art of writing was developed in Egypt. It is conceivable that legend crept in, because nobody can tell stories for hundreds of years and keep all of the facts straight. They couldn't do it then, and they can't do it now. The only way that you can keep facts altogether straight is to write them down as they happen, and then preserve the writing. So that, to give you an analogy of what I'm trying to say to you, if someone would tell you tonight a story of an incident that took place during slavery, that involved some kind of brutality to the slaves, I'm sure you could not conceive of that story being factual in every detail. (Does this make you sleepy? I saw a lady yawn and I was wondering if it made her sleepy. I was hoping that you were listening with interest to what I am trying to say. Listen if you please.)

Now, here is a story that we do not question its spiritual meaning. We do not question altogether its historical meaning. But the religious value, the spiritual value, is there. It shows the humanity of Noah. Noah was, after all, a man; and, of course, he responded like other human beings. Some people forget that, and think because Noah or Abraham or Isaac or Jacob lived at another time, and the Bible records many incidents in their lives, that they were not human—but they were; they were.

In this particular story, frequently it is used by segregationists as an example of why the Negro is black. They make Ham the ancient ancestor of black people, and, of course, they make the other sons, Shem and Japheth, the ancestors of other racial groups. But, first of all, I want to say that there's nothing to this interpretation of that story, because Ham is not the ancient ancestor of black people. And black people are not black because God cursed them because Ham saw his father naked, drunk and naked. In the first place, this is historically wrong, for in terms of history it does not set the story in its proper perspective. Thus it is historically wrong, because I'm sure that there were black people way before Ham. (You don't hear me.) Thus it's historically wrong.

It is anthropologically wrong, that is, in terms of the science of man. In terms of anthropology that deals with the science of man, it's wrong, because man did not come to his racial characteristics, color, etcetera, by somebody's curse. Hmm? For you can't curse anybody; and what is more than that, God would not empower you to curse your brother. Hunh? You may cuss him, but you can't curse him. (You didn't hear me.) I said you may cuss him, but you can't put a curse upon him by divine sanction or by divine authority. For if God is the God of love, and if God is the God of justice; if God is the father of all men, what father would give another child, another one of his children, the power to place a curse upon another one of his children, and his children's children's children? What kind of God would that be? (You don't hear what I'm saying. I want you to pray with me.) Thus it is not only historically wrong, but it is anthropologically wrong. It is also theologically wrong, because it is inconsistent with the religious philosophy of theology, and thus it's wrong.

And then, another thing I want to say to you, we are black, not because we are cursed, for blackness is not a curse; it is a curse only if you think so, and, you know, it's not really a curse then; it's just the way you think. Blackness, so far as God is concerned, so far as truth is concerned, is just the same as whiteness; for God has all kinds of colors in his world, in his universe, and he has not condemned any color. All colors are beautiful in the sight of God. (You don't hear what I'm talking about.) And the only reason why you entertain a thought like that is because you have been culturally conditioned by white people to think that way, and they conditioned you that way because they used this as a means to an end, to give you a feeling of inferiority, and to then take advantage of you, socially, economically, and politically.

Color ain't got nothing to do with it. The part of the world from which you came is responsible for your color. You lived in a tropical situation originally, where the sun was severe, and generations of heat effectuated the color that you are now. If you have a broad nose, it is because nature did that, in order that your intake of oxygen would be great enough for you to survive; because in the kind of intense heat that you came from, out of that part of the world from which you came, with a thin, closed-up nose, you couldn't have lived. Your oxygen intake would not have been sufficient for survival. Don't have nobody tell you—. You know the word *atoma,* from which we get our word *atom,* means earth, earth. You know, out of the dust of the ground, God created us? So atoma, from which our word atom comes, means earth. Now whoever's seen any white earth? Hmm? If man came from the ground, you understand, it seems like original man couldn't have been white. So people are white, also, because of the part of the world from where they came originally: the frigid zones, the cold zones determined all of this. It had nothing to do with a curse; it had nothing to do with God authorizing somebody to curse us, and, you understand, that color is a mark of the curse—nothing is further from the truth, if you understand it within its scientific context. And, of course, the Bible says a certain situation arose and Moses' hand turned white. Now if Moses was already white, how did his hand turn white? Hunh? Nobody but somebody dark could have a white hand? That is, speaking of it in this sense; because there would be no need to speak of his white hand if his hand was already white. (You don't see what I'm talking about.)

So there was no curse; it was no curse. And the word Adam does not mean a person; it means man. It means man. Just like the word Negro does not mean a person; it means a whole group, doesn't it? When you speak of "the Negro" you're talking about Negroes in general. Thus the word Adam has the same meaning originally, so let's get this out of our minds that God would empower one of us to curse another, that God would give that kind of advantage to one of his children over his other child. He is a just God, I believe. Someone asked me one night, after preaching, "Reverend, if God is just, then why do we have wars? What about the things that happen to us? Why were we so mistreated when we were slaves?" God has nothing to do with that. God made man a free, moral agent, and gave him the ability to choose good or evil, right or wrong. So if a war comes on, and millions of people are killed, it's not God, it's man. The world order is responsible for that. Because Hitler killed millions of Jews was not responsible to God; it was responsible to Hitler and the German people.

But, then, although God gives you the ability to choose good or evil, he doesn't make you do either. But what he does do, once you have chosen, you must be responsible for your choice. (You don't hear what I'm saying to you.) You must suffer the consequences, as Germany did, and as America is doing today. You may not know it, but we are suffering the consequences of our former or historical choices. Now, I think it would have been terribly wrong if God would have had given to a drunk, naked man the power to curse one of his own grandchildren because he was mad with his daddy. (You don't hear what I'm saying.) Now, he's going to come up out of a drunken stupor and put a curse on his grandchildren and their grandchildren and their grandchildren and all down through history—this doesn't seem logical, does it? No, sir. Noah was responsible for getting drunk, and Noah was responsible for getting naked. (You don't hear me.) And Noah had to suffer the consequence of having chosen to get both drunk and naked. Now, this is attributable to Noah's humanity, Noah's weakness, Noah's finiteness.

Although Noah had done many good things that people don't take time to talk about—they would rather talk about the bad things, for people are just made up like this. You can go to the hospital, and visit with the sick; you can go to the home of the sick and take care of it until they get out of the hospital; you can preach people's funerals and marry them; and you can baptize them and you can do all kinds of creative, good things; [and] nobody's going to make a headline out of that. (You don't hear what I'm saying.) Nobody's going to put themselves to the trouble to get on the telephone and talk for hours about the good things that you did. You can do good things for a year or even twenty years or even thirty years, forty years; after forty years of good things, do one wrong thing and they will talk about that far more than all the good things that you did for forty years. (I wished I had somebody here to pray with me. Listen.)

I remember reading a story about a young man who was a member of one of the professional ball teams in the major leagues. And this young man was their home-run king. He had played on the team for a number of years,   [whooping:]

and
>   he had brought,
>   as it were,
>   the bacon home.
> He was their
>   star,

and

whenever they got in trouble,
        they always called on him,
and

usually
        he always came through.
And

when he would do this,
        the team
        would mob him
        with admiration.
O Lord.

But one day,
after bringing them victory
        and making them champions for years,
o Lord,

he went to the bat,
and

the team
        was in a tight.
They said,
        "Come on, now,
and do like you've always done,
        to get us out."
And

the young man
struck at the first ball
        and missed it.
The crowd laughed
        with admiration;
said, "He's just fooling around;
        wait on him a little while."
Well,

the pitcher wound up
        and threw another ball.
The batter struck at it,
        and missed it.
O Lord.

His teammates
        and the crowd
called out,
"Quit playing now,
and come on,

give us a home run."
O Lord.
"The bases are loaded,
and we are counting on you.
If you'll bring in those boys
on the bases,
and bring yourself in,
you'll put us out in the lead."
But when the last
ball was pitched,
why,
the batter went down
swinging.
O Lord.
They got angry with the young man,
yes they did.
They got angry with him.
They said, "He let us down."
O Lord.
He let us down today.
But someone said,
"Don't you remember
how many times
he lifted you up."
O Lord.
"No,
I'm not talking about that now,
I'm talking about he let us down,
today."
O Lord.
And they threw him
off the team,
yes they did.
And let me tell you,
I think the same thing applies,
where Noah is concerned.
O Lord.
Do you remember
that Noah did some noble things
before he got drunk one time?
Yes he did.
Noah preached
one hundred and twenty years.

Why didn't somebody say something
            about that?
O Lord.

Noah,
according to the story,
preserved
            and saved his people.
Why didn't someone
say a good thing
            about that?
And then there's another thing.
Noah
            walked with God.
            Noah walked with God.
He was a man
that appreciated
            divine presence.
He had divine awareness.
Why doesn't someone
            say something about that?
O Lord.

The world,
the universe,
is full of good.
Yes, there is evil,
but there is also good,
and I believe that good,
is stronger than evil.
O Lord.

Men will
fight wars,
men will
shoot one another down,
men will
take advantage of their brothers,
but I believe
that good will be victorious
            one of these days.
One of these days.
Oh!
One of these days.
Oh, one of these days.
There's going to be a homecoming

when you come home one night,
yes,
yes! yes!
God will be victorious
one of these days.
Yes!
I know he will tonight.
Yes!
Yes.
I wonder do you see what I'm talking about.

[Speaking:]   Good will overcome. Good will overcome. Good
will triumph. Good will be victorious one of these days. [Singing:]

For I want to tell you,
God is not dead.
God is not dead.
      God is not dead.
Let the war clouds rage,
and,
    let the storms [?] rage,
I want you to know,
that God is still on the throne,
      yes he is.
He's still on the throne. He's still on the throne.
Like the little girl
on the train one night,
when the train was racing along the tracks,
and everybody was afraid,
the little girl set down in the aisle,
playing with her doll,
and somebody said, "Little girl,
don't you know danger is imminent?"
The little girl said, "I'm not worried.
My father,
my father,
my father,
    is the engineer."

[Speaking:] My father is. I'm not worried. My father's in charge of
this train, this train of life. God is the engineer. He overrules and super-rules
in the affairs of men. God bless you.

18

A Bigot Meets Jesus

[*The Conversion of Paul*].
Jewel LPS 0079.
Recorded ca. 1973.

In the book of the Acts of the Apostles, we read the following, beginning with the third verse of the ninth chapter of the book of Acts: "And as he journeyed, he came near Damascus: and suddenly there shone round about him a light from heaven: and he fell to the earth and heard a voice saying unto him, Saul, Saul, why persecuteth thou me? And he said, Who art thou, Lord? And the Lord said, I am Jesus whom thou persecuteth. It is hard for thee to kick against the pricks. And he trembling and astonished said, Lord, what would thou have me do?"

A bigot meets Jesus. A bigot.

Now, before we attempt to interpret this text in a sense of relativity, that is, related to our own lives and our own experiences, let's see what a bigot is. If we don't get that straightened out, then you won't know what kind of person I'm talking about. I said a bigot meets Jesus.

A bigot is a person who has no respect, no sympathy, no concern about any religion or any creed or any person or any race except *his* religion, *his* creed, *his* color, and *his* race. He's intolerant to anything else but that which *he* approves. Now, we hear a great deal about bigotry among whites, and this is true; many of them are bigots. But then, at the same time, we find that there are bigots among us. We find intolerance, a lack of understanding and a lack of appreciation, a lack of approval among us, except they come up to what we have had decided: they should come up to the standards that we have set. Such a person has a closed mind; such a person is misguided. A person without tolerance and without open-mindedness toward other people who differ from them in race, in religion, or anything else is a bigot. And you find that kind of person among black people, white people, brown people, red people—they're bigots.

But I said here, after reading this passage, this bigot happened to meet Jesus. His bigotry was exercised in the realms of religion. He was Jewish in terms of his religion; he was Hebrew in terms of race. Now, anybody else that did not meet those standards was not tolerated. He did not subscribe— (shake those people that you see asleep next to you; this is no sleeping room here. I see three or four people across here asleep!)—may I say that the man to whom I refer's name was Paul. That is, his English name was Paul, translated from the Greek, *Paulus,* and prior to that, his Jewish name was Saul. Being an exclusive Jew who did not approve of other people except they were Jews, [he] did not associate with them, did not visit with them. If they went into their homes, or their countries, or their cities, they would go through certain cleansing ceremonies, like shaking the dust from his feet at the border. And, except they were Jews, they were Gentiles or heathens. As I said this morning, it's a funny thing, that when you don't meet the approval or measure up to the standards that some people have set for you, they'll call you, they'll put all kinds of labels on you.

This bigot, this Jew, this exclusivist, this segregationist, happened to meet Jesus. Let me tell you how it was. I think something had been going on in his mind sometime prior to this experience. He witnessed the stoning. Imagine stoning being a religious act! Throwing stones, putting a person down in a valley there somewhere and three or four or five hundred of you get up there and go to throwing stones down on you. Isn't it funny how much brutality and how much viciousness that people can do in the name of religion? There are some people who call themselves Christians and who have decided that you were wrong because you were not a member of his church, of his religious persuasion. They can cut your throat and feel like they're doing right. They can crucify you, or assassinate, so to speak, your name, your character, your reputation, and feel like they're doing right. "Oh, honey, he's not right, nohow." (Laughs.) Well, you're certainly not right by hurting me.

Anyway, he witnessed the stoning of Stephen; he saw how humble and how willing this man was to accept his fate, which was motivated by their blindness and their ignorance and their closed minds. And while they stoned him to death, in the process he lifted up his eyes toward heaven and told God to forgive them. This man saw on the face of that man something that he had never seen before. Stephen was stoned because he embraced a new interpretation that Jesus gave to God; and these people, the high priests, and Paul and all the others, had sent out orders to find these Christian devils.

The Christians, as you know, were known first as the Galileans; and then secondly they were known as the People of the Way; and at Antioch they became known as Christians. (I ain't got nobody praying with me here tonight. Listen.) I said this man witnessed a unique something in the character of Stephen, under a hail of stones, and death was imminent. Now, he had to leave, or take up stoning, when he got up a little older, but he never did forget this Stephen thing. Now, when he became trained and embraced Judaism, and went to the top echelon of Judaism and became a Pharisee, he went on to carry on the persecution of the Christians. But as he was assigned to go 140 miles to Damascus, looking for Christians, with his deputies by his side, he rode along, leading them. (I'm a little hoarse; pray with me. I got a cold. It's been so cold here recently I got a little cold. Pray with me. Listen.) As he neared Jerusalem, he heard a voice. Hmm? It's a funny thing that [if you are] one who embraces God, you can hear things with people all around you, that they can't hear. Hmm? He heard a voice. It's funny that nobody in the crowd heard the voice but Paul. He heard a voice. Oh, I think the old people who used to join the church years ago, they didn't know too much about religious philosophy, they knew very little about theology, you know; their English was not always correct: but their feeling was up to par. They claimed that they heard voices; they heard voices. No wonder the hymnologist said,

> I heard the voice of Jesus say,
> come unto me and rest;
> lie down, thou weary one, lie down,
> thy head upon my breast.

Listen. I want to tell you that you can hear voices. You can hear voices, now, you can hear voices. He speaks to me sometimes, right now. Sometimes, when I'm in a crowd; sometimes when I'm alone; I hear his voice. I hear his voice. So Saul, or Paul, claims that as he rode along that road, as he neared the limits of the city, he heard a voice and he swears that it was from heaven. For you can differentiate between a voice from heaven and a voice from somewhere else. You can differentiate between these voices.

Now, the next thing he said, he saw a light. (You don't hear me.) He saw a light; he saw a light. Look here. No wonder the Christian boasted that "He led me out of darkness into a marvelous light." If you didn't see a light—I don't mean an imaginary light; I don't mean that—I mean, if a light of a new understanding has not broken forth in your life, if you cannot see right from wrong in relation to your fellow men, if you cannot see, when you are tempted to take advantage of me, or your brother or your sister, then there's no light in your life. There's no light in your life if you can't see that. And a man who was born of God can hear voices and can see lights. And he'll walk in that light, that beautiful light. (You don't hear me tonight.) Yes he will. And Paul claimed that the light that he saw was brighter than the noonday sun. Oh, it is bright. It is bright. It's brighter, the light from heaven *is* brighter than the noonday sun. For, you see, there are some things that I can't see by the light of the sun. (Did you hear me?) I said, there are some things that I can't see by the light of the sun, but by that light from heaven I can see things

that I've never seen before, I can understand things that I've never understood
before because I'm looking at those things in the light from heaven that has
broke forth in my life and has lighted up my understanding, my compassion,
my sympathy. Oh yes, I know what Paul was talking about when he said he
heard voices and he had seen the light. Yes, he was a bigot and in his early
age he joined mob crowds. He witnessed mob scenes so long until he became
a mobster himself. (You're not praying with me tonight.)   [Whooping:]

You know
        another man
                that saw the light
                and heard the voice.
        [They] tell me,
                that at the time
        that he heard the voice
                and saw the light,
that
        he began writing
                a new song:
        "Amazing grace,
                how sweet it is,
                how sweet it sounds,
        that saved
                a wretch like me;
        I once was lost,
                but now am found;
                was blind
                but now I see."
O Lord.
        This man's name
                was John Newton.
        But this other mobster,
        this John Newton,
great God,
        was a pirate
                on the high seas.
        He robbed ships
                of their cargo;
        he killed other sailors
                for selfish gain.
(You don't hear me.)
O Lord.

And

      I said when a man
           encounters Jesus,
      it's a revolutionizing
           experience.
      You can't
           hear those voices
      and see the light from heaven
           and remain the same.
(You don't hear me tonight, do you?)
O Lord.
And

      Paul
           said,
      when he heard it,
           he was convinced
           that it was the voice
           of a superior being.
      He didn't know
           who he was,
      but he knew
      it was necessary
           to address him as "Lord."
O Lord.
      "Lord,
      what would thou
           have me to do?
      I've never met you before,
           but I know you're Lord.
O Lord.
      I've never encountered
           another experience before
           but I know you're Lord.
O Lord.
      I know
that
      you're a superior being
      and somehow
           that I ought to subscribe to you
           and I ought to
           dedicate my life to you.
O Lord.

O Lord,
what would thou
            have me do?"
O Lord.
Well,
        you know,
        thank God,
that
        the Lord
        does not take
                    our jobs from us.
O Lord.
        He said to Paul,
        "Keep on,
        go to the same place
                    where you went before,
                    or where you were headed.
        You just go there,
        look for the man
                    that you intended to destroy,
        and let him tell you
                    what I would have you do."
O Lord.
        (You don't hear me tonight.)
        O Lord.
        "O Lord,
        what would you have me do?"
Great God.
        I believe tonight
        that that's the first thing
        that I wanted to know
                    when he touched my soul.
        That was the first thing
        that when that light from heaven
        shined on me,
        the one thing I wanted to know was,
                    "What would you have me do?"
O Lord.
        "O Lord!
        Here are my hands!
        Here are my feet!
        Here are my eyes!

Use them as if they were yours.
O Lord!
What would you have
     me do?"

[Speaking:] What would you have me do? What would you have me do? You that's outside of the church tonight ought to ask that same question: "Lord, I surrender all, and what would you have me do? What would you have me do?"

19

Meeting Jesus
in the Dawn

[*Fishermen Drop Your Nets*].
New Bethel Baptist Church, Detroit, April 30, 1978.
Field recording by Jeff Titon.

Consider now the book of St. John, the twenty-first chapter, beginning at the third verse. "Simon Peter said unto them, I go fishing. They say unto him, We also go with thee. They went forth and entered into a ship immediately; and that night they caught nothing. But when the morning was now come, Jesus stood on the shore: but the disciples knew not that it was Jesus. Then Jesus said unto them, Children, have ye any meat? They answered him, No. And he saith unto them, Cast the nets on the right side of the ship, and ye shall find. They cast therefore and now they were not able to draw it for the multitude of fishes. Therefore that disciple whom Jesus loved said unto Peter, It is the Lord."

It is the Lord. I want you to think about that now, because there are some experiences that we can have that make us know at once that it is the Lord. Didn't know him at first [laughs], but after certain things transpire, after going through the process of certain experiences, when we thought that those experiences were devastating to us, or on the brink of being ruined, but as they worked out they turned out just the other way, and we have to come to the conclusion that it is the Lord. For he does do things in mysterious ways; and sometimes to start out, we don't understand what he's doing.

Well, this passage, this appendage was added to the book of John by whoever that John was. Some of us who are limited in our understanding of critical theology ascribe John the apostle as being the writer of the book of John, but upon looking on it and examining it critically, we know that it could not have been John the apostle, because John the writer was a conversant and able Greek scholar. He starts the book off talking about the *logos,* a philosophical concept where God had translated himself into human terms and reduced himself to the point that we could see and appreciate him. So it wasn't John the apostle, for they were not scholars, they were not learned men; they were ordinary people as we are.

Now the purpose that this writer, whoever the John was—some said he was a member of the church at Alexandria—but whoever he was, we know his purpose for adding this story in the last chapter of his book. It was to certify the fact of Christ's resurrection.

There had been some stories floating around. The women said that they mistook him one morning after the crucifixion for the gardener. Another group said that they were going to Emmaus one evening, kind of getting out of town, dodging the Jerusalem police, and they wanted to get out inconspicuously. Therefore they didn't go in a crowd. But on the way they met Jesus and he walked along the highway with them and they persuaded him to come in and sit down. And they way he broke bread, they knew it was the Lord. Another report was that he appeared to a lot of people on the last occasion on a mountain range in Galilee.

Then there was a report that came out that they told Thomas, that "You weren't at the meeting the other Sunday, and Jesus was there." Thomas said, "Well now, I don't believe that because there is no record of any man from Adam to now that has escaped the claws of death. No man, no man. Read your history. Examine your experience. And see if you can come up with one that has escaped the clutches of death." And Thomas said, "More than that, I'm scientific in my thinking and I'm not going to be swept by all of these winds and doctrines. If any of you have seen Jesus, it was a ghost or spirit. It was hallucination or he was a spirit and I'm not going to believe it, not only about him, about anybody else. Unless I see the nail prints in his hands and unless I examine the sword marks in his side, I'm not going to believe it." And they said that on the second meeting Thomas was there, [and] with the doors being closed, Jesus walked in. And it is said that he said to Thomas, because he read Thomas's mind, he knew Thomas's thinking, and he challenged Thomas on his contentions. "Now, Thomas, here are my hands. Thomas, here's my side." And Thomas fell down and said, "My Lord and my God." [Jesus] said, "Thomas, you're just believing because you have had a chance to see and examine, but blessed are those who have not seen and yet have believed."

So they said, "Since there are a lot of you who've been calling Jesus a spirit or ghost, or that we were suffering hallucinations, we were letting our imagination run away with us, we want to tell you another story. Peter and the other followers were sitting one day idle. We were watching the fishers, the fishermen, go to the lake as they had been doing for centuries. Been three years since we'd been out. And of course Peter, after much thought, much disillusionment, feeling lost, feeling their dream had gone up in smoke and had come down to ashes, Peter said, 'I don't know what you all are going to do, but I'm going back to my old trade. I'm going back to fishing.' "

And you know when you suggest anything about going backwards, you can always get a crowd. (I don't believe you hear me.) You can always get a crowd if you talk about going back, if you talk about going backwards, if you talk about retrogression, you've always got some followers. And said to them, when Peter said and the others said, "We'll go with you," [it] seemed like the whole idea of the kingdom of God and its realization had already faded.   [Whooping:]

It
        seemed like
that
        we're beating
            a dead horse
            so to speak.
So
        "I have
            my family,
and
        I'm going back
            to my old trade."
But you know
        sometimes
            we can stray
            from the original calling
            and for what is destined
            in our lives.
        Jesus had said,
            "Drop your nets
            and follow me."
O Lord.
        But Peter said,
            "He's dead.
And
        I saw him
            when he dropped his head
            and said, 'It's finished.'
O Lord.
        I saw
            them take him down
            from the cross
O Lord.
        And so there
            is no reality
            in the idea anymore.
And
        I'm going back

    to my boats.
  I'm going back
    to the lake.
  I'm going back
    to my nets,
yes I am."
And
    they said, "We'll go with you.
O Lord.
  Well,
  what about
  all of those
    appearances
    that have been reported?
  What about the women?
  What about Peter?
    And what about the boys
    on the way to Emmaus?"
O Lord.
  "Well, maybe all of us
    have made a mistake.
O Lord.
    And I'm going back."
  But you know when you go backwards
    in your life,
  when you retrogress
    in your life,
o Lord,
  you'll find yourself
    floundering around.
  You'll find yourself
    making fruitless efforts.
  You'll find yourself
  running into one thing
    after another.
O Lord.
  So, tired,
  weak and worn,
  worn out from weariness,
  they rowed in
    to shore that morning,
and
  they saw a man

standing on the shore
in the dim dawn.
O Lord.
He called out to them
and said, "Have you caught anything?
Have your efforts been rewarded
in your all-night toil?"
And they said, "No, Lord.
We've toiled all night
and caught nothing."
O Lord.
Jesus said,
"I'm standing where I can see
a school
or a shoal of fishes.
O Lord.
Ohh, drop your net
on the right side.
Your trouble has been
you've had your net
on the left side.
You've had your net
on the wrong side.
Ohh.
Ohh drop your nets
on the right side."
Ohh yes.
And
as soon as success came,
they said,
"It's the Lord.
It's the Lord.
I knew it wouldn't have happened
if it hadn't have been for the Lord."
Ohh well,
ohh well,
I know it is the Lord.

[Speaking:] I know that so many things would have happened to me
if it had not been for the Lord. I know that I would have been dead and in my
grave if it had not been for the Lord. I recognize him just like John did.
Sometime, when things happen to me, I have to say, "It's the Lord." God
bless you.

20

A Mother
at the Cross

New Bethel Baptist Church, May 14, 1978 (Mother's Day).
Field recording by Jeff Titon.

I want to talk with you this evening from a passage found in the book of St. John, the nineteenth chapter, the twenty-fifth and the twenty, through the twenty-seventh verse. "Now there stood by the cross of Jesus his mother, and his mother's sister, Mary the wife of Cleophas, and Mary Magdalene. When Jesus therefore saw his mother, and the disciple standing by, whom he loved, he said unto his mother, Woman, behold thy son! Then said he to the disciple, Behold thy mother! And from that hour the disciple took her unto his own home."

Now I want to talk about a mother at the cross. I think the thing that makes us identify ourselves with Jesus is because of his humanness. I thank God that he didn't make him without the tendency of temptation. I thank God that the Lord made him in such a way that he got hungry, he got tired, he got sleepy, he got lonely. He wept, cried like you cry sometimes.

In this instance he did something very characteristic of himself, that under the spell of excruciating pain, in an hour when he felt like even God had forsaken him, when darkness was not only upon him physically but darkness was upon him mentally and spiritually. We have those hours sometime with us, for in our lives some rain falls, some winds blow, some storms arise. But characteristic, characteristic of him because under those unusual circumstances he thought about others: he thought about his mother.

Now his mother had been with him from birth. She was at the cradle, she was in the home, she was in and out of the carpenter's shop. She walked backwards and forward to Jerusalem along with him. Those were not hard places, bad places, but the thing that makes this experience unique is that she was not only at all of these other places, she was at the cross. (I don't believe you're praying with me tonight.)

She was at the cross. Now there are some theological commentators who said that while Peter had denied him and many of the others had deserted him and Judas had betrayed him, Mary was there—. Some of the commentators say that she was there because she was permitted to be there under the cultural situation, that women were not thought of as equals in anything: in responsibility or anything else. It is said that women were almost unnoticed. But this is a sad commentary.

Anytime a man has been charged with treason—hmm? Anytime the Roman government has ruled that you are guilty of treason, it's dangerous for anybody to be with you. (Did you hear me?) Anytime the Jewish church had decreed that he was a heretic, an impostor, and a devil—I want to tell you, it was dangerous for Mary to be there.

You know, if you've read this Scripture with any care, the Scripture surrounding the trial and crucifixion of Jesus, the arrest, the trial, and the crucifixion, you'll notice that the charge was first a religious charge. He had blasphemed against God, according to the high priests. But the country, Judea, although the Jews had some rights, they did not have the right of capital punishment. (Did you hear me?)

And of course when they came up with that charge, Herod wouldn't deal with it. "Now you've got to get us another charge. Now whatever he's done to offend you-all here in your church, we can't deal with that. It's certainly not deserving capital punishment. If you want him put to death you got to come up with a better charge than that." And they went back and brought up treason, saying that he was working against Caesar. He was working against the state. He was inspiring and instigating a revolution against Rome. Then Caesar said, "Well now—" or Pilate said, "Well, I can deal with that now. If he's, if he's doing anything against the state, then we can deal with him."

Now I'm trying to say that through it all, Mary was there. His mother was there. Jesus, I mean Cecil [Franklin] talked about the qualifications of a mother this morning, and motherhood was not just something biological, but is something that one has to earn. Just because you have had a child doesn't make you a mother! Motherhood is something that one has to achieve. Well, I'm trying to tell you that Mary was a model mother. She not only brought him into this world, she taught him the traditions of his people. She saw to it that he observed all of the rites, all of the ceremonies. And here at the end, she was there. Didn't have the privilege of being at his bedside. It was worse than that. She was standing by his cross.

Say, "Well, why wasn't she scared?" Love rules out fear. Say, "Well, he has broken the law." Love doesn't care anything about breaking the law. Some folks say, "I love you when you're right, but when you're wrong I'm through with you." Then you don't love. (You don't hear me.) Because if you love me, you're with me right or wrong. You're there to help me get strength if I'm wrong.

She was at his cross. Her sister was there, and then Mary Magdalene was there. Her sister, who was the mother of James and John, had come to him one day and said, "Well now, I know that you are going to follow the Messianic tradition and I know you're about to get your kingdom set up and organized. I want my two sons to be closest to the throne. I want James on one side. I want John on the other. Don't have too much time to worry about other folks' children; I'm talking about mine." Jesus pointed out to her the selfishness of her ambition but it didn't crush her, for she was working for her own children; she was functioning as a mother. (You don't hear me tonight. Listen if you please.)

I believe it was Rudyard Kipling who said,

If I were hanged from the highest hill,
    Mother, o mother of mine;
I know whose love would follow me still,
    Mother, o mother of mine.
If I were damned—or drowned, rather, in the deepest sea,
    Mother, o mother of mine;
I know whose love would come down to me,
    Mother, o mother of mine.
If I were damned of body and soul,
    Mother, o mother of mine;
I know whose prayers would make me whole,
    Mother of mine, o mother of mine.

She was at the cross. I tell you, if one is in the deepest sea, she's there or her prayers are there. If you're damned body and soul her love and prayers will make you whole. (You don't hear me.)

So Jesus said, "Woman," which was not derogatory, considering it within the framework of his culture. It was not disrespectful. He said, "Woman, behold your son." Said, "Now I know I'm about to leave here. I'm hanging from a tree. And my weight is tearing the flesh in my hands. But I want to see that you have a home before I leave here. I want you to have somewhere to go. Now I've got some brothers but I can't leave you with my brothers because they don't believe in me." (I wished I had somebody here to pray.) "I want to leave you with somebody who believes that God has wrought a miracle in my life." (You don't hear me today.)

That was one of the things he said from the cross. Another one, I said he was concerned about others, another one was, "Father forgive them, for they know not what they do." And then, "Verily I say unto thee, today thou shalt be with me in Paradise." And then, "Father, into thine hands I commend my spirit." These were things that he said while he was dying.

Somebody said he stopped dying long enough to run revival and take one of the thieves along with him. (You don't hear me.) Stopped dying and prayed for them, and said, "This day you'll be with me in Paradise." And then he said, right after he appointed Mary a home, "I thirst. I've been out here since noon, hanging on this tree. I've been out here under unusual tropical sun. I've been losing blood since last night. But I wanted to get at least one of the thieves straight. And then I wanted to pray for everybody who's doing things against themselves and others. I wanted to pray for them before it's over. And then I want to commit and commend my spirit to God." And certainly he did. And when he said that, he dropped his head, and said, "It's finished. The battle is over. The task has been completed. The work has been done. To this end was I born. [Whooping:]

And

    for this cause

        came I

        into the world.

And

    it's finished now.

O Lord.

    I don't need

        anybody

        to commit me.

    I don't need

        anybody

        to read the burial ceremony.

Well

    I'm going to say it

        myself.

Yes I am.

    Into your hands

        I commend my spirit.

O Lord."

And

    I remember reading

        a story a long time ago

        that dealt with

    mother's eternal love.

    It is said

        that her son

was in jail,
and he was in there
because he had been condemned
to die.
O Lord.
They were going to put a rope
around his neck
and
the hangsman
was going to remove
the plank on which he was standing.
O Lord.
And
they
had tried
and failed
time and again
to get him a reprieve.
O Lord.
And every time
they failed.
O Lord.
The mother
thought about an old
tradition
that went on and obtained
in that country:
before they hanged
anybody
they had to ring the bell.
O Lord.
And early that morning
she got up
and went down
to the courthouse
where
the gallows had been situated.
O Lord.
She climbed up
in the belfry
about an hour
before time.

O Lord.
    And
    then the hangman
    and his crowd
        came marching out.
And
    she was up in the belfry
    holding on
        to the bell clapper.
O Lord.
    They got the rope
        in their hands.
    They pulled down
        but there was no sound.
    And as they pulled the bell,
    the bell swung over
        from one side to another.
O Lord.
    She fell
    against the iron wall
        of that big bell.
    O Lord.
    She was bruised,
    she was bleeding,
    but she held on
        to the bell clapper,
    oh yes she did.
    Yes.
    And after awhile
        they gave up.
    After awhile
    they said, "Since the bell won't ring,
        we can't execute him."
O Lord.
    By that time
    she fell down
        upon the ground
        under the bell clapper
    with blood
    running from her nose,
    from her eyes
        and from her shoulders.

O Lord.

> She said, "Well, son,
> I know you meant good.
> You are my child.
> Go on.
> Don't worry.
> Don't worry
> about me.
> I'm all right."
> O Lord.
> Did you know
> that Jesus,
>> Jesus
> held the bell clapper
> of time and eternity
>> in his hands?
> Oh well,
> ohh,
> yes!

Afterword

As literature, the Christian sermon dates from the apostolic age. Throughout the Middle Ages many of the church fathers—St. Augustine, for instance—turned the sermon into a learned work of art that must be composed by rules. From the Middle Ages through the seventeenth century, Europeans were exposed to sermons more than any other literature. Far from being dry, scholastic exercises, the early sermons contained generous helpings of allegory, fable, dialogue, and drama. Sermons were the most widely printed genre from the invention of printing to the start of the eighteenth century, but with the rise of the scientific worldview, printing of sermons declined until now very few outside the religious establishment consider sermons to be literature of any importance. The standard literary anthologies in English include only the sermons of John Donne and Jonathan Edwards.

The decline of the printed sermon among Europeans and white Americans coincided with the rise of the African American sermon and the production of an oral literature of considerable merit and great cultural importance. When Africans in the United States took on certain aspects of Christian belief and practice, exhorters and preachers arose among them. Two traditions emerged. Reports of black preachers from the latter half of the eighteenth and early nineteenth centuries emphasize the oratorical skills of freedmen such as "Black Harry" (Harry Hoosier, d. 1810), who traveled throughout the United States with Bishop Asbury and was "reputed by some to be the greatest orator in America";[1] Richard Allen, who founded the African Methodist Episcopal Church in 1816; and Andrew Marshall, pastor of the First African Baptist Church in Savannah, Georgia, from 1812 to 1856. Some of these freedmen preached from manuscript, others without notes; many were praised for having "sonorous" voices.[2] In contrast, slave preachers or "exhorters" were not given

to oratory so much as to vivid, imaginative, extemporaneous, dramatic retell-
ings and reenactments of Bible stories, particularly from the Old Testament,
often having to do with Jewish heroes who overcame oppression—allegories
of their own situation. In the more intimate setting of the slave quarters, the
congregations—almost always wholly black—shouted and prayed and sang in
response as the preachers delivered their messages. And at the early nineteenth-
century camp meetings, where both blacks and whites were in attendance,
these slave exhorters effectively ministered to the African Americans, often
after the whites had retired for the night.[3]

After Emancipation, African Americans continued to organize and
direct their own churches, chiefly Methodist, Baptist, and, later, Pentecostal.
The two streams of preaching continued: the learned orators were seminary-
trained, preached before large, urban congregations, and were well connected
in the denominational hierarchy, taking part in the politics of the state and
national church organizations. The other stream, derived from the slave exhorters, has been variously described as "old-time Negro preaching,"[4] "spiritual"
preaching,[5] and "performed" preaching.[6] It is most commonly referred to as
"folk" preaching,[7] on the grounds that the preachers and congregations are
more or less "ordinary folk" rather than representative of the black elites, and
that the sermons are the stuff of folklore, for many of their subjects and themes
have been passed down through the years orally from one preacher to another.
Many view the folk preacher as a vanishing phenomenon, but the fact is that
the folk sermon is one of the most vigorous forms of African American
folklore, and the folk preacher is scarcely an endangered species. Although
she avoids the term *folk,* Portia Maultsby argues that the folk tradition was
"independently developed by Blacks, utilizing the concepts and practices
retained from their West African heritage." The learned orators belong to the
other tradition, one heavily influenced by white Protestantism.[8] Reverend C.
L. Franklin deliberately tried to combine the best of both traditions.

Early black ministers and churches published sermons for local con-
sumption,[9] but the first more widely available collection may have been
"Brudder Coteney's Sermons," Gullah Negro sermons edited by John G.
Williams.[10] The next seems to have been William Hatcher's *John Jasper*
(1908), a group of folk preacher Jasper's sermons transcribed in dialect by an
admirer.[11] *God's Trombones,* by James Weldon Johnson, was published in
1927 and offered "Seven Negro Sermons in Verse."[12] Johnson wrote these
poems "after the manner" of the folk sermons.

To Johnson, an astute observer, the old-time preacher was a poet, for
he was "a master of all the modes of eloquence." With an imagination "bold
and unfettered, he had the power to sweep his hearers before him; and so
himself was often swept away. At such times his language was not prose, but
poetry."[13] The proper medium for presenting sermons like these in print,

Johnson felt, therefore was poetry. He called attention to the accentual rhythms, the syncopation, the audible breaths at the ends of lines—these he indicated with dashes—and, above all, the intoned chanting so characteristic of the old-time preacher, and asked the reader to supply them in his mind's ear. Because the preacher was "saturated with the sublime phraseology of the Hebrew prophets and steeped in the idioms of King James English," his language was not Negro dialect but "a fusion of Negro idioms with Bible English; and in this there may have been, after all, some kinship with the innate grandiloquence of their old African tongues."[14] To my knowledge, Johnson was the first to set the sermons as poems, and he did so in free verse. In her 1935 collection of folklore, *Mules and Men*, Zora Neale Hurston offered an excerpt from a folk sermon; and in her novel *Jonah's Gourd Vine* (1934) she made a folk sermon the centerpiece and presented it in full.[15] But like Johnson's, these sermons were literary re-creations in free verse, rather than authentic sermons.

Hurston, along with John and Alan Lomax, recorded authentic sermons in the 1930s for the Library of Congress's Archive of Folk Song. One of the Lomaxes' recordings, an Easter sermon delivered in prison by "Sin-Killer" Griffin, was later released on a Library of Congress record album and is still in print. The sociologist Charles S. Johnson recorded nine sermons for Fisk University,[16] and the Julius Rosenwald Fund sponsored a two-year study by John Henry Faulk on black folk sermons in Texas. In prose and in Negro dialect he transcribed many of them for his 1941 University of Texas M.A. thesis, "Quickened by de Spurit." Alice Jones's 1942 M.A. thesis for Fisk University was entitled "The Negro Folk Sermon: A Study in the Sociology of Folk Culture." In 1951 William H. Pipes, a professor at Fort Valley (Georgia) State College, published *Say Amen, Brother!*, a study of black folk preaching in Macon County, Georgia, that included prose transcriptions and lengthy analyses of seven sermons.[17] Bruce Rosenberg's pioneering 1970 book, *The Art of the American Folk Preacher*, showed how the chanting preachers make use of oral formulas and themes in order to compose their sermons at the moment of delivery, a technique used by Homer and oral epic singers the world over.[18] With this effort, Rosenberg brought the folk sermon to the attention of literary critics. He has written a number of incisive articles on the folk sermon since then, the most recent an analysis of the sermonic techniques behind Jesse Jackson's moving speech at the 1984 Democratic National Convention. In 1985, Gerald Davis published *I Got the Word in Me and I Can Sing It, You Know*, offering a penetrating and celebratory appraisal of the African-American-ness of the folk sermon style, a scholarly reinterpretation of the use of oral formulas, and an aesthetic model for the successful sermon.[19] His excellent documentary film, *The Performed Word*, captures black folk preaching in a wider African American context. And several useful general books on African American religion[20] and an insightful discussion of black preaching[21] came as the result of religious ferment in the black communities occasioned by the Civil Rights Movement and Black Power Movement.

Commercial recording companies issued 78-rpm discs containing "sermons with singing" from the 1920s to the 1950s. These studio recordings are not to be confused with the real thing, but they do offer authentic singing and a glimpse, at least, at some of the themes and preaching styles. And the records sold very well: sales of the Reverend J. M. Gates's sermon records in the 1920s were exceeded in the black "race" record market only by Bessie Smith's blues records, and among black people old enough to remember his records, Reverend Gates's name is well known. As a boy, Franklin listened to Gates's records at home. Some of the commercial sermons seem to have been designed as much for amusement as spiritual uplifting—Gates's later sermons are a fair example—and this source material, valuable as it is, must be used by scholars with caution, whereas Franklin's sermons are simply recordings of what went on in his church. When Franklin's sermon albums entered this market in the early 1950s, they came with the force of a revelation. Many others followed in his wake, but his were by far the most popular.

As the Civil Rights movement developed, Franklin aligned himself with Martin Luther King, Jr., and in 1963 he invited King to accompany him in a civil rights march in Detroit. King accepted. They drew two hundred thousand people and King read the same speech he read later that summer in Washington, *I Have a Dream*. Franklin was a member of SCLC, and later joined PUSH, Reverend Jesse Jackson's organization; but national political activism per se took a backseat to his chief missions, preaching, pastoral care, and local politics, as he led New Bethel through the turbulent sixties. Many important black political figures, including Detroit mayor Coleman Young, Michigan congressman John Conyers, Detroit city council president Erma Henderson, and state senator Jackie Vaughan, were close to Franklin and campaigned in New Bethel, which meant reaching hundreds of thousands via Franklin's radio broadcast. And he preached topical sermons on such subjects as black power and the importance of black history.

In 1968 he preached at the Poor People's Campaign, organized in Washington by SCLC. A contemporary account describes his enormous impact:

> Friday night a Campaign mass meeting was held at St. Stephen's Baptist Church, where the church was full and the crowd unusually boisterous. The featured preacher of the evening was Rev. C. L. Franklin of Detroit. Rev. Franklin is the father of Miss Aretha Franklin, a very successful soul singer, and he was an old friend of Dr. King. A solidly built man with sleek shiny hair and a booming voice,

Rev. Franklin was a real master of the black Baptist preacher's art. . . .

"I hope I can get somebody to pray with me tonight," he began, warming them up, "because you know, I'm a *Negro* preacher, and I like to talk to people and have people talk *back* to me." He paused while they roared their pleasure. "I want to talk to you tonight about 'They Wouldn't Bow.' " [A version of *The Fiery Furnace,* Chess LP-35.]

Franklin's delivery crossed the line between speaking and singing as he rose toward a crescendo, and the responses from the crowd became tumultuous and almost continuous, beyond hope of reproduction in print. The roots of his famous daughter's vocal style could be heard reverberating in his voice. At the climax he suddenly turned and sat down, leaving the crowd in mid-cheer. . . .

It was a magnificent performance, unequaled during the Campaign in brilliance of delivery or frenzy of response. It was the closest the Washington mass meeting ever came to the kind of exultation that makes a movement the center of a community's attention.[22]

In the 1970s Franklin stopped his preaching tours and concentrated on his New Bethel ministry. The congregation fell to about three thousand—still a large church, one of the largest in Detroit—and Franklin received the recognition due him as the elder statesman and father figure. I think now of Franklin's own father, who left Mississippi just after Clarence was born and joined the American troops in Europe during World War I. Coming back after the war, he felt that sharecropping in Mississippi was too confining. He left and Rachel remarried, and Franklin had had his problems with his stepfather, running away from home, returning and eventually over his stepfather's objections choosing to preach, not to plow. In the picture of God as a loving father he found an image and model of a wise elder, a strong and benevolent and loving presence who would be a constant companion.

Franklin's image of God was undeniably masculine. Women adored him, but they appeared in his sermons as types: the nurturing mother, the temptress, the fallen angel, the faithful servant. He viewed motherhood as woman's highest calling, and he preached Mother's Day sermons about Hannah and Mary as ideal mothers, teaching their children the traditions of their people, loving and caring for their children no matter whether the children did right or wrong. In so doing he was drawing on his own experience, for he credited his mother with raising him as a Christian. But although he accepted women preachers and early on allowed them to preach from his pulpit (a radical position within his denomination), and although he preached in support of women and aided them in the church and in politics, he did not, to my knowledge, preach in support of the Women's Movement. His sentimental attitude toward women drew on Victorian middle-class values as they penetrated African American culture, and it was reinforced by his continuing friendship with his mother. Certainly, he understood that times were changing, and that black women deserved fair treatment and equal rights no less than black men. But they also deserved special protection. The Christian tradition he carried was thoroughly patriarchal, from Adam and Eve on down; it was this Bible that he studied, and it was this tradition that he preached. His sermons were peopled with masculine heroes; and it is clear that his image of the heroic figure was masculine.

It is not easy to sum up Franklin's legacy as a preacher, but his place in the history of the black American church is secure, while his sermons cry out for a wider audience. He was, after all, one of the masterful poets of this century, and it is only a matter of time before this recognition comes his way. As I have suggested, the African American sermon is a combination of argument (spoken oratory) and faith (chanted poetry). For the believer, the prose language of the church—oratory and the language of the Bible—permeates daily life, shapes daily thought and utterance. The language of faith, the cry to God in prayer, the sermon's "whooped" poem, is on the other hand an extraordinary, ecstatic response to the mysteries of faith, and it thrusts the believer back into the source of belief, feeling the power of God. Making and remaking black folktales as the stuff of his sermons, Franklin told and chanted stories to both ends, oratory and poetry, and his sermons stand as exemplary, both as expressions of the black American experience and as a human response to his own struggles and to the struggles of his people.

NOTES

1. Henry H. Mitchell, *Black Preaching* (Philadelphia: Lippincott, 1970), p. 69.
2. Ibid., p. 72.
3. Albert J. Raboteau, *Slave Religion* (New York: Galaxy, 1978), pp. 135–36; John W. Blassingame, *The Slave Community*, rev. ed. (New York: Oxford University Press, 1979), pp. 130-31; Sidney E. Ahlstrom, *A Religious History of the American People* (New Haven: Yale University Press, 1972), p. 703.
4. James Weldon Johnson, *God's Trombones* (1927; rpt. New York: Compass, 1969), pp. 1-11; William H. Pipes, *Say Amen, Brother!* (1951; rpt. Westport, Conn.: Negro Universities Press, 1970).
5. Bruce Rosenberg, *Can These Bones Live?* (Urbana: University of Illinois Press, 1988).
6. Gerald L. Davis, *I Got the Word in Me and I Can Sing It, You Know* (Philadelphia: University of Pennsylvania Press, 1985).

7. Langston Hughes and Arna Bontemps, eds., *The Book of Negro Folklore* (New York: Apollo, 1958); J. Mason Brewer, *American Negro Folklore* (New York: Quadrangle, 1968); Johnson, op. cit.; Harold Courlander, ed., *A Treasury of Afro-American Folklore* (New York: Crown, 1976).
8. Portia K. Maultsby, "The Use and Performance of Hymnody, Spirituals and Gospels in the Black Church," *Journal of the Interdenominational Theological Center* 14 (Fall 1986/Spring 1987):141–59.
9. Davis, p. 40.
10. John G. Williams, *De Ole Plantation* (Charleston: Walker, Evans, & Cogswell, 1895).
11. William E. Hatcher, *John Jasper* (New York: F.H. Revell, 1908). Jasper's most celebrated sermon, "The Sun Do Move!," was published in New York in 1882 by Brentano's Literary Emporium.
12. Johnson, op. cit.
13. Ibid., p. 5.
14. Ibid., p. 9.
15. Zora Neale Hurston, *Mules and Men* (1935; rpt. New York: Harper Perennial, 1965); Zora Neale Hurston, *Jonah's Gourd Vine* (New York: Lippincott, 1934).
16. Pipes, p. 3.
17. Ibid.
18. Bruce Rosenberg, *The Art of the American Folk Preacher* (New York: Oxford University Press, 1970); revised as Rosenberg, op. cit.
19. Davis, op. cit.
20. See, for example, Leonard E. Barrett, *Soul-Force* (Garden City, N.Y.: Anchor, 1974); C. Eric Lincoln, ed., *The Black Experience in Religion* (Garden City, N.Y.: Anchor, 1974).
21. Mitchell, op. cit.
22. Charles Fager, quoted in Charles V. Hamilton, *The Black Preacher in America* (New York: William Morrow, 1972), pp. 29–30.